I LOVE

WHEN

THAT HAPPENS

by MAY THE

SCHWARTZIE
BE WITH YOU

Library of Congress Control Number: 2019930119
ISBN: 978-1-949639-18-6

Cover Design: Miguel Parisi
Interior Design: Megan Elger

TABLE OF CONTENTS

FOREWORD

For years, my father dreamed of writing two books. One would be a memoir of his life, full of stories about his childhood and adolescence, his early years in Chabad Lubavitch, his career as a campus rabbi, and his innovative work in The Chai Center of Los Angeles. The other he saw as a volume on theology, philosophy, and Jewish teachings.

He actually began work on the memoir in late 2015, long after his diagnosis of the disease that would take his life. Renting an office space away from home, he began to gather decades of emails, essays, newspaper clippings, and photographs. He wrote up a few short chapters—but then his condition worsened, requiring chemotherapy that left him even more debilitated. He made a couple of audio recordings that could be transcribed, but he had to give up the project before it got off the ground.

After Schwartzie passed away in February 2017, I reflected on how much he wanted to write his memoir and how much he had to offer to readers, and, as the son who had worked by Schwartzie's side for fifteen years, I decided to make his dream a reality. Along with other family members, I started to amass years and years of materials, including Schwartzie's personal emails, e-blasts and other communications from The Chai Center, physical artifacts and hard copies of letters and documents, recordings of his speeches, and videos, both serious and lighthearted, showing Schwartzie at work and at leisure.

Although we turned over electronic copies of everything we collected to a firm that facilitates the process of turning such material into book form, it's important to note that this book was put together to reflect what Schwartzie would have written had he been able to complete the project.

Ninety percent of the text is from Schwartzie's point of view, in his voice. A small part comprises testimony from family members and other people who knew Schwartzie. Third-person narration is used occasionally to introduce or to bridge, but nothing was made up. The bulk of the book comes from my father's own writings: his reminiscences, his communications, his speeches.

This, I think, is the book Schwartzie would have written if his time on Earth had been longer.

Coming from a family that contains at least one hundred adults and a circle of friends and associates who number many more than that, I know that once this book is published, I'll be receiving many questions that begin, "Why didn't you include the story about _____?" One answer is, if I included all the stories people suggested, the book would be 600 pages long. But the more important answer is that not all of the stories that were part of my father's rich, productive life suited the purpose of this book.

Schwartzie started life as a typical postwar Jewish boy from an observant but not Orthodox family—a Jewish kid like thousands of others. But he undertook a spiritual journey by which he became not only a leader among Jews, but a unique presence in his community of choice. He had many connections among the film, television, and music industries of Los Angeles, and this book could have contained many stories about Schwartzie's interactions with this or that celebrity. But those stories don't speak to Schwartzie's life purpose, which was to foster involvement with Jewish ritual, bring Jewish people together, and help ensure a Jewish future. The stories I included are meant to entertain, but mostly to inspire you, the reader.

I created this book as part of my father's legacy: in equal parts joy, inspiration, devotion, connectedness, awe, and love.

Mendel Schwartz
Los Angeles, December 2018

IN THE BEGINNING

The Early Years

CHAPTER 1

VIENNA, AUSTRIA: FLEEING THE NAZIS

Before there was Schwartzie, even before there was Shlomo, there was Bobby.

I remembered a childhood unlike those of my classmates in school. I grew up jealous of all the *goyim* in my neighborhood. Every birthday, my friends had grandparents, uncles, aunts, and many cousins with whom to celebrate. On my birthday, no one came. We had no family. Everyone had been killed in the Holocaust.

I was born on November 12, 1945, the seventh day of Kislev, in Atlantic City, New Jersey, to Cantor Morris E. Schwartz and his wife, Frances (née Gewürz), Hungarian Jews who had settled in Vienna before fleeing to the United States. Born Moshe and known in Austria as Moritz, my father Morris sang at the Storchenshul Synagogue in Vienna, while Frances, a skilled corset maker, was proprietor of the Vienna Corset Shop, a business she and Morris would reopen in Atlantic City. They had three children. My oldest sibling, Olga, was born in 1925, Greta in 1927, and the love of their life, their only boy, Sammy, in 1928.

The Schwartz family was in Vienna when Austria was annexed by Nazi Germany in March 1938, and my parents began to plan their eventual escape from Europe, moving to Budapest, Hungary, and placing their children with different relatives in Hungary and Yugoslavia.

As soon as the Nazis occupied Vienna, they found the president of my father's synagogue, brought him up to the roof of the synagogue, and pushed him off, killing him. They tried to make it look like a suicide.

Ten minutes after that murder, they knocked on the door of my father's home, asking for Herr Ober Cantor Schwartz. By coincidence (but there are no coincidences!), he wasn't home. When my father returned, the family packed up two generations of belongings and the members ran for their lives.

My parents were able to liquidate their assets and get their money out of Austria through the intervention of a friend, Catholic priest Anton Röder. My father subsequently obtained an affidavit from a relative in Chicago promising sponsorship, and because his birthplace was at the time part of Czechoslovakia, he was granted a visa under that country's quota—fortuitously, because the Hungarian quota had been filled. The American Embassy tried to send him to the United States alone, but my mother argued that as an experienced corsetiere, she was more likely to find work than her husband, who would be looking for a pulpit among a glut of liturgical singers. The embassy agreed but would not allow them to bring over their three children, then ages ten, twelve, and thirteen, until mother and father could show that they were earning a living.

After stops in France, England, and Ireland, my parents left Europe in March 1939, expecting to have their children with them within a few months. My father enjoyed an early windfall when a synagogue in Pitts-burgh paid him $1,000 to sing High Holidays services, and he gave the Hebrew Immigration Aid Service (HIAS) the money to get his children out of Europe, where World War II had begun. My mother found low-paying work in a factory that hired refugee workers, and my father, also desperate to show long-term prospects for employment, signed a contract with a synagogue in Atlantic City at the exploitative salary of $25 per week.

They had to contend with government bureaucracy and with HIAS staffers who ranged from incompetent to corrupt. An official "misplaced" the money my father had paid for steamship tickets for the children, and even after months of inquiries, my parents were not allowed to speak with a more senior official. Finally, Mom waylaid the HIAS president's secretary and threatened to attack her with a pair of scissors unless she gave my mother the president's home address and telephone number. When she confronted the president in his penthouse apartment, he promised to look into the matter the next day, but Mom would not be denied. Finally, the president consented to go with my mother immediately to his office and check the file for the tickets. The clerk responsible had taken the money and conveniently misfiled the file. The matter was immediately taken care of by the apologetic president.

My three siblings, Olga, Greta, and Sammy, arrived a few weeks later on one of the last American liners to leave Europe before the borders were closed. My parents were not reunited with their children until May 1940, by which time they had been separated from their parents for almost 14 months. Less than two weeks after their arrival, the U.S. State Department effectively cut off immigration of Jewish refugees from Nazi-occupied Europe. Almost every member of my parents' extended families perished during the Holocaust.

My parents acclimated themselves as quickly as they could. Mother reopened her store under the same name it had in Austria, the Vienna Corset Shop, and ran it for almost forty years. Father conducted High Holiday worship for hundreds of Jewish GIs at Convention Hall to serve military personnel at local bases. He supplemented his meager salary conducting Jewish lifecycle events and teaching; when he had learned enough English, he trained as a mohel. His hope was to move to a larger, more sophisticated city where his talents would be appreciated.

Frances Gewürz and her corset shop in
Vienna, Austria

Cantor Morris Schwartz
and his choir

Receipts of Payments for Travel Expenses.

1939 advertisement for Cantor Morris Schwartz's High Holidays services

My sister Gretta's ship tickets to the US, 1940, issued to "Margit Schwartz"

Morris and Frances, Olga, Gretta, and brother Sammy, and cousin Ella Nussenzweig murdered by the Nazis in 1944

Morris Schwartz's mohel certificate

8

CHAPTER 2

FROM TRAGEDY TO UNLIMITED JOY

Tragedy struck the family in 1943, when my brother Sammy, then thirteen and a stellar student, was struck and killed by a taxi while riding his bicycle on an icy road.

My sister Greta wrote:

> *After Sammy's sudden death, my father became deeply depressed and rebelled against his religion. He could not find an answer to this tragedy which took his only thirteen-year-old son, nor to the tragedy of losing his entire family in Europe. To watch my father's world shattered by the loss of his only son was agonizing. His "Kaddish," the son to carry his name, his pride, his hope, his future.*

The truth is, my brother Sammy was an only son, the Schwartz my parents were counting on to bear our family name into the future. It was devastating.

But a miracle came about that revived the family: my mother, Frances, age 43, conceived another child—me.

It certainly seems that if my brother hadn't been killed, I would never have come into existence. At first, it was thought that my mother had a tumor, but she insisted that she felt life within her, and she delivered her last child by Cesarean section. I was named Shlomo Yitzchak for my paternal grandfather, who was shot to death shortly after the Nazis occupied Hungary in 1944. My English name, Robert, honored my grandmother Rivka Sara, who also was killed by the Nazis. The only package she walked into the concentration camps with was her *tachrichin* (white shrouds).

Everybody called me Bobby.

Greta wrote:

If a prince were born, he could not have been loved or spoiled more openly than my brother. My father, who always had been reserved, suddenly changed into the most doting, tolerant father. He had never touched a child in diapers, but now he bathed, fed, and diapered his son. He was an expert at doing this. The open love he showed his son was fully returned. Soon, screams for Daddy were heard all over the house.

Compared to my early upbringing, very little discipline was practiced on this beautiful, blond, perfect child. To quote my father, "Now joy and laughter entered the house again." There was a renewed energy to live for, and great plans were made for this young prince. Nothing was too good for him. This was a true Yankee. American born, he could even become president of the United States. My father mellowed greatly, and his strong beliefs returned. He stopped questioning and accepted.

I love that.

My sisters adored me and my parents found happiness again. By the time I was born, my family had moved from an apartment to a house in a pleasant section of Atlantic City. When my sisters, who were eighteen and twenty years older than I, had children of their own, my name went from Bobby to "Uncle Bobby." So, from the time I was eight years old, all my friends and classmates called me Uncle Bobby. When I was sixty years old and visited some of my old buddies, they still called me Uncle Bobby. When the whole world called me Schwartzie, my classmates still called me Uncle Bobby.

My family was more observant than most Atlantic City Jews were—not quite Orthodox, but traditional. The synagogue at which my father made his career didn't have a *mechitzah* (partition between men and women during prayer), but men and women sat separately. In a Jewish community of eight thousand, I remembered only two Jewish-owned stores closed on Shabbat, one of them the Schwartzes' Vienna Corset Shop. There were only two kosher butchers, no kosher restaurants, and no Jewish day schools: every Jewish child attended public school. In Vienna, our family would have been categorized as fiercely ultra-Orthodox. As it was, through most of my childhood, neither I nor my father wore a *kipah* (yarmulke) on the street, or even at the dinner table, except on Shabbat.

TYPICAL AMERICAN JEWS

"We both grew up as typical American Jews. Not terribly identified, certainly not what could be labeled Orthodox," said Steve Bailey, today a retired professor of clinical psychology, who met Bobby in third grade and went through public school, Hebrew school, and yeshiva with Schwartzie. "We got into minor trouble, like all adolescents do. Smoking under the boardwalk, and I think just little, not terrible things, but mischievous things, like everybody did. We were both normal kids. I remember Bobby as always mischievous, always with a sense of humor, and always popular. And yeah, he was a good-looking kid."

Bailey, whose family also lived in the same neighborhood as the Schwartzes' and attended their synagogue, Chelsea Hebrew Congregation, remembered Bobby's parents as hard workers. "His father worked in the store, aside from being the chazzan. He was sort of a tough guy, not the typical sort of European father, pushing his kid very hard to succeed. His mom was a typical European, Hungarian mother. Very nice, a very Jewish-mother kind of person. Both of them were strong characters, and just mostly preoccupied with the business and making ends meet.

My family came to an educational crossroads when we started seventh grade in the late fifties. At the point when we had to switch over to junior high school, they bused all of us kids from the Italian-Jewish neighborhood to a black neighborhood in the mid-city, which presented a problem for many of us white kids. We were beaten up very often and got our lunch money stolen, and it was not a good social situation in the public school. It was here that I met my first crush, a nice Catholic Italian girl named Frances Ginnetti. She had a twin sister named JoAnne, so we orchestrated for my best friend, Steve Bailey, to get the smarter girl. I got the prettier one, and we double-dated for weeks. My father got wind of this new relationship as we began to openly date and stroll the boardwalk together on Sundays. Father told me, "If you don't sever ties with her, I will cut you out of the will. You will receive a one-dollar bill." I'm not sure how much was in his will, but I saw my father was extremely stern and very much pained. I obeyed my father and broke off the relationship.

The father of the rabbi of our synagogue was on the board of Talmudical Academy of Baltimore at the time, and the rabbi suggested that I, along with some of my friends, should be sent to Baltimore to study at the yeshiva. We were twelve years old, and it was kind of difficult to leave home, but that was the only option.

My father worried that I would suffer living away from home so young, but he also wanted me in a more Jewish environment. People told my father, "Your son looks and acts like a *goy.*"

So, Steve and I, products of a mediocre after-school Hebrew program, had to acquire some of the background and experience in traditional text study that Orthodox day-school boys usually bring to yeshiva. Happily, one of our Hebrew school instructors, Bernard Steinberg, an immigrant from Czechoslovakia, volunteered to teach us some basics. He wasn't a rabbi, but he was educated. He taught us how to read Rashi and introduced us to what Mishnah was and a little bit of Talmud. We went every morning at six to the synagogue for an hour of instruction, and then we left for school. We did that for a whole year.

We were too young to live in the academy dormitory in Baltimore, so our parents arranged for us to live with rabbis on the faculty. Thus it was at age twelve that I entered a world of Jewish teaching and practice entirely new to me at Talmudical Academy in Baltimore, Maryland.

I'm second from right

My home in Atlantic City

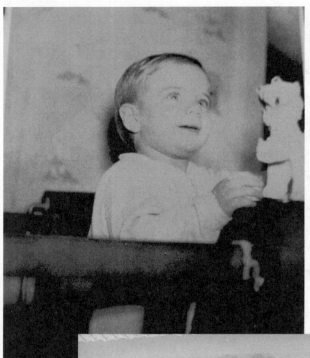

Baby Bobby with his teddy bear

I'm the tough guy on the left

With my father, Morris

Ring Bearer

Pogo Stick

TALMUDICAL ACADEMY

In the fall of 1958, Talmudical Academy (TA) of Baltimore was located in Park Heights, then a solidly Jewish neighborhood. Founded as the Hebrew Parochial School in 1917, TA was a model of the modern Jewish day school from its inception, encompassing not only yeshiva-style study of sacred texts, but also modern Hebrew and secular subjects. Rabbis at the school, many of whom had studied and taught at great European *yeshivot*, conducted classes in Yiddish.

That's where I arrived, still three months short of my thirteenth birthday, with Steve Bailey and a third Atlantic City boy. We were housed and began classes, but with a serious impediment.

When we came to TA, we basically had a background. The only thing we didn't have was that neither of us could understand and speak Yiddish. The teachers, the ones who taught the upper grades, taught only in Yiddish; it was problematic.

Steve dealt with the issue differently than I. In the beginning, he sort of sat there and didn't know what was going on. Neither of us knew what was going on. But I, you know, couldn't sit still and do nothing. So, I started to behave in a way that got me kicked out most mornings from class, and then both of us had to go and find out what was taught that day. We had to learn at night, and somebody taught us what happened that day in class. But, of course, that didn't help us the next day, because we still didn't know what was going on.

I got the reputation of being the troublemaker and the comedian, which I became very good at. I could imitate any of the rabbis perfectly, which became the source of tremendous entertainment for all the rest of us. I was so good at this that I was invited to do a Purim spiel (a holiday comedy skit) at our rabbi's home and make fun of all our teachers and the faculty, including our own teacher, who was our host. The rabbi's wife was present among all the students. She was in stitches. She couldn't get enough. The rabbi didn't find it humorous at all, and I was forced to apologize to him.

Eventually, after about six months, I picked up enough Yiddish to be able to know what was going on, and it went on from there. But I retained my funny, extroverted personality the whole time I was there. I was told later that I was not considered a serious student, as many of the others were, but I was fun to be around and fun to be with. Good enough.

"I remember that most of the time that I saw him during those five years at TA, he was in his pajamas," said Dr. Abe Genut, one of my classmates, when we were much older. "He liked to sleep late."

By the time I was living in the dorm, my high jinks were getting on the TA rabbis' last nerve. After two years, the school administration informed my father that the staff didn't want to admit me to the school for the next year. They told him that I was on the basketball court more than I was in school, plus other various and sundry infractions.

In a last-minute effort to try to get me back into the school, my dad drove almost four hours to Baltimore from Atlantic City and had a meeting with me, the dean, and the dorm supervisor, Rabbi Milikowsky, whom everyone adored because he really cared about each individual boy, including me. My father tried, but the dean wasn't having it.

Finally, Rabbi Milikowsky spoke up. He knew that if I didn't get back into the school, then I was headed for Atlantic City High School and would be fully assimilated into the secular world by the time I graduated. He said that he would take me into his home for the upcoming school year. He had a bunch of kids who were young and living at home.

The dean was livid. Right then and there, he said to Rabbi Milikowsky in a loud, threatening voice, "That means that every time he gets into trouble, I'm going to call *you* into my office, and *you* will be responsible for your 'jewel' and his violations."

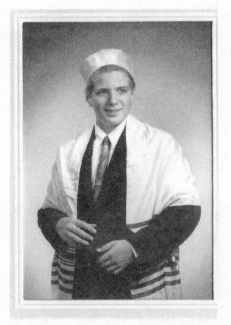

Cantor and Mrs. Morris Schwartz
request the honour of your presence
at the
Bar Mitzvah
בר מצוה
of their son
Robert I.
שלמה יצחק
who will conduct the Services and read
the Law and Haftorah
on Saturday morning, November twenty-second
nineteen hundred and fifty-eight
at nine o'clock
Chelsea Hebrew Congregation
Dover and Atlantic Aves.
Atlantic City, N. J.

Hildan Jay
Atlantic City, N. J.

Standing proudly with my two gorgeous, blue-eyed, blond Austrian sisters

Signature of Parent

First Report...... *Rev. Morris Schwartz*

Second Report...... *Rev. Morris Schwartz*

Third Report...... *Rev. Morris Schwartz*

Fourth Report...... *Rev. Morris Schwartz*

PROMOTION RECORD

Date..................

Promoted to Grade..................

Heb. Teacher..................

Promoted to Grade..................

Eng. Teacher..................

"Not Theory But Practice Is The Major Aim Of Study"

ישיבת חפץ חיים דבלטימאר

TALMUDICAL ACADEMY OF BALTIMORE

COTTAGE AND SPRINGHILL AVENUES

BALTIMORE 15, MARYLAND   Liberty 2-7311

JUNIOR AND SENIOR HIGH SCHOOL

Progress Report

	Heb. Gr.	Eng. Gr.	School Year
Name: Schwartz, Robert	9	9	59-60

Off. Teachers: רבי א. פישקין, Hebrew: Rabbi D. Fishel

English: John Nappe

The Talmudical Academy endeavors to give its students a thorough Hebrew and secular training, and to imbue them with the lofty ideals of Torah and good citizenship.

Good work habits and excellent attendance are the keys to successful achievement. It is, therefore, essential that you give these two sections of the report card as much attention as you give to achievement.

Cooperation between the home and school is essential in the educational process. This report card's value will be enhanced greatly if it is studied carefully with your child before signing and returning it. For further information regarding your child's progress, consult with the principal and teachers.

HEBREW SUBJECTS

		1st Report	2nd Report	3rd Report	4th Report
Reading	קריאה	90	95		A
Writing	כתיבה	80	85		
Language	עברית				
Chumash	חומש	85	88		B
Rashi	רש"י	80	84		B-
Prophets	נביאים	80	85		B+
Prayers	תפלה				
History	הסטורי				
Laws & Customs	דינים	85	89		B+
Music	זמרה				
Talmud	גמרא	85	89		B+

HABITS AND ATTITUDES

	1st Report		2nd Report		3rd Report		4th Report	
	Heb	Eng	Heb	Eng	Heb	Eng	Heb	Eng
Health Habits								
1. Keeps neat and clean								
2. Maintains good posture								
Study and Work Habits								
1. Shows initiative								
2. Plans work well								
3. Does careful work								
4. Follows plans and directions								
5. Begins work promptly								
Effort								
1. Is industrious								
2. Completes assignments								
Citizenship								
1. Is courteous								
2. Respects property & rights of others								
3. Works & plays well with others								
4. Observes school regulations								
5. Takes active part in group activities								

ENGLISH SUBJECTS

	1st Report	2nd Report	3rd Report	4th Report
English	C	F	C	C+
French				
Hebrew				
Latin	B+	C+	C+	D
General Science				
Biology				
Chemistry				
Physics				
Mathematics				
Algebra	A	B+	B	D+ C+
Geometry				
Adv. Algebra				
Trigonometry				
Art				
Hygiene				
Physical Ed.				
Music				
Social Studies	C+	C	C	C

ATTENDANCE

	1st Report		2nd Report		3rd Report		4th Report	
	Heb	Eng	Heb	Eng	Heb	Eng	Heb	Eng
Days Absent				1		5		10
Days Tardy				0		0		0

* Summer 1960 - Friends School Atlantic City, N.J.
English I - Algebra I

COMMENTS

Hebrew Teacher..................

English Teacher: *Has good potential but not working to maximum 12-59. His conduct must improve*

CODE:

A	E — Excellent	C	F — Fair		
B+	VG — Very Good	@	P — Poor	P	
B	G — Good	@	D — Deficient	F	
		L — Progressing on his own level			

A report card from Talmudical Academy when I was still a class clown

My senior yearbook from
Talmudical Academy

Talmudical Academy

CHAPTER 4

HASSIDISM

The Tanya and Rabbi Itche Springer

I more or less stayed out of trouble during my last couple of years at TA, when my spiritual focus kicked up a notch and I began spending significant time with Chabad, then in the first years of its proactive outreach with emissaries.

According to my pal Steve Bailey, my involvement with Chabad began with music. "Bobby had a great voice," he said. "He liked singing, and he liked to go there for Shabbat, and to go there to daven because of the singing, and he started to get interested in the philosophy of Chasidut."

Perhaps an even bigger draw was Itche Springer, the first really charismatic rabbi I had ever met.

Rabbi Yitzchok Springer had been a Chabad emissary in Baltimore for several years and was still under thirty years old when I met him. Born into an observant Polish family, he survived World War II in Siberia and became swept up in the Chasidic movement after the war. Following a stint in the Chabad community in the new state of Israel, he received permission to visit the Lubavitcher Rebbe and traveled to New York in 1954. Springer became part of the community at 770 Eastern Parkway, the global headquarters of Chabad Lubavitch, in Crown Heights, Brooklyn.

After he learned English, he was sent to Baltimore, where he scratched out a living teaching, lecturing, and selling holy books, attracting many Jews to Chasidut.

"He looked like a stereotypical aloof Chasid, but he was an absolute doll," said Schwartzie's son-in-law Jacob Shallman. "He loved Judaism and G-d; he was authentic, happy, and kind. Poor as hell and happy as can be."

Springer taught a late-night class on the *Tanya,* a foundational text of Chasidic philosophy that serves to this day as a kind of life manual for Chabad Chasidim. The administrators at TA, followers of a different strain of Orthodoxy, didn't particularly want their students hanging out with Chabad.

The dean of the yeshiva banged on the table one morning after the prayers, and he said, "Anybody who goes to Rabbi Springer's Chasidic *Tanya* class is expelled from school." I saw this prohibition as a challenge. I didn't know why, but I figured if it isn't allowed, it's a good thing. So I found out where the class was and I went.

"They were not people who had warm feelings toward Chasidut and Chabad," Steve Bailey said of the Talmudical Academy rabbis, though he didn't think it was that big an issue at the school.

"They felt he was being influenced a bit too much by Chabad during the last couple years, but it didn't cause any real crisis or any tension."

Rabbi Springer's class led to my increasing involvement with Chabad and may have been the thin edge of the wedge that eventually separated me in terms of study from the non-Chasidic yeshiva world. That tiny class that the dean of the yeshiva told me not to go to was the undoing of my connection with the regular yeshiva life. That's how I became religious and joined the Chabad Lubavitch movement.

It was all positive, because he taught us some of the songs and some of the Chabad *nigunim* (wordless tunes), and my friend Steve and I went to Chabad events. Chabad makes you feel good and happy, so there was nothing negative going on. Some of our buddies went to have a good time; some went for the songs. I took the learning of Chasidut much more seriously.

It was Rabbi Springer who suggested that I spend some time learning at Chabad headquarters in Brooklyn the summer before I entered Yeshiva University in Manhattan with a cohort of boys from TA. By then, my predilections for Chasidut—and sleeping late—were well documented: the Robert Schwartz page in my high school yearbook featured a cartoon of seventeen-year-old "Uncle Bob" sitting up in bed, in his pajamas, with a suitcase on the floor next to the bed marked "770 or Bust."

Robert Schwartz

יפוצו מעינותיך חוצה

My page in the yearbook. The Hebrew quote states, "He will spread the teachings of Torah to the world."

Uncle Bob, as he has been affectionately nicknamed, has been placed here, we feel, to produce happiness among the sad and to put smiles on the faces of the troubled. His effervescent spirit and his warmth blend perfectly to endow him with the rare gift of humor. He has an uncanny talent for the right joke at the right time, which has broken up many a class discussion.

The other side of Bob is that of the understanding and concerned friend who is always prepared to come to the aid of anyone who may need it. It is certain that Shlomo, one of Rebbi's favorite *Talmidim*, will be most successful in the Torah world.

Author of the Tanya – Schneur Zalman of Liadi

Itche Shpringer

CHAPTER 5

EXPRESS TO BROOKLYN: BEATNIKS VS HASSIDIM

By the early 1960s, Yeshiva University (YU) in upper Manhattan, the flagship academic institution of modern Orthodoxy, had adopted *Torah u'madda*, "Torah and secular knowledge," as its motto. YU should have been a good fit for me.

It wasn't.

My parents and siblings had been poor during their first years in the United States. But by the time I was attending school in Baltimore, my parents were able to send me to college, and they wanted me to go to a school in which I could start training for a profession.

> *"He wasn't an immigrant. He was a Yankee. He didn't speak with an accent. He got all the American cultural references," Schwartzie's nephew Ron Reisman reported. "At some point, the Schwartz family thought that he would become a lawyer. So, when Bobby went to Yeshiva University, his parents believed they had raised a religious kid who would lead an otherwise secular (that is, prosperous and professional) American life."*

I dutifully accompanied ten of my Talmudical Academy classmates to matriculate at YU in 1963. They called us the "Baltimorons."

But by then, Rabbi Springer had introduced me to the joyous, immersive life and liveliness of Chasidism.

> *"Bobby was a round peg in Yeshiva's square hole. He felt he didn't fit in," Reisman said. "He was not satisfied—at a basic level—at YU."*

In my late teen years, I was at a crossroads. I had completed the first semester of my freshman year at Yeshiva University. It certainly seemed that the next three and a half years were going to be the same as the first very depressing six months. I had made many friends who weren't so religious, and I was on the fence about how religious I would become.

I would hang out in Greenwich Village in the pre-hippie days, riding the subways at all hours of the night. Members of the counterculture movement then were called beatniks. They would play the bongo drums and recite poetry. Bob Dylan was playing in clubs in the Village for small audiences, before he became *Bob Dylan*. We drank espresso and cheap rot-gut wine. I'd say *l'chaim* with gentiles. That whole group was quite friendly.

About once a month, I went to Brooklyn to spend time with the happy and colorful Chasidim. They were even happier than the beatniks. I would hear the Lubavitcher Rebbe's Shabbat talk at the *fabrengen,* a joyous gathering of Chasidism that lasted all afternoon. Basically, I was going back and forth for a year between the Village and Crown Heights.

I wrote an eight-page letter to the Rebbe on why I should come to Lubavitch, drop YU, and abandon my father's anti-Chasidic opinions and go to Newark Yeshiva, which was the Lubavitch hub for study at the time.

The Rebbe answered, *"Hakol tulei b'haskamas uvicha:"* Everything depends on your father's consent. Knowing that my father would not consent to this newfound way, I went to the Lubavitch teachers and asked them what to do. They said I should listen to the Rebbe and ask my father, and the Rebbe will do his part. When I went home to Atlantic City to address my father on this explosive topic, my father gave me his consent.

Only after my father's consent did I mention my letter to the Rebbe and his reply. My father said in Hungarian to my mother, "I hold of this Rebbe very much," and then walked out of the room. I asked my mother to explain what had just happened. My mother told me, "Your father was very upset that he was losing his son to the Chasidim and wrote a letter to your Rebbe. He explained in his letter to the Rebbe, complaining of his son's current circumstance, and was very distraught, especially since he did not like or agree with the Chasidic viewpoint." My mother told me that my father was further upset because he had never even received a response from the Rebbe. Nothing. Not a letter, not a phone call. My father was very impressed, however, upon hearing from me that the Rebbe had told me that everything depended on my father's consent. This was an answer to me, and was also an answer to my father's letter, and it caused my father to change his mind.

I remember an occasion in 1964, when I came to a gathering at 770, celebrating a new arrival from the Soviet Union. The Rebbe wasn't present, just the Chasidim. Asher Sasonkin was the Chasid who was recently released from the Soviet Union and was holding court late into the night. One story Asher told that night greatly captivated me. It was after many years with Asher as a prisoner in Siberia; there was a new, young commander who took over the management in that particular Siberian camp. He was proving to the staff how capable and ruthless he was. He commanded Asher the Chasid to shave his beard, or by the next morning he would have two soldiers do it for him. When Asher said no, he was put into solitary confinement for three days. The floor was wet, cold, muddy, and infested with lice and rats. The ceiling was too low for Asher to stand.

Asher told us that night in 770 that when he was released from solitary confinement, "*Baruch haShem* (praised is the Lord), they didn't touch my beard." Asher said this with the biggest smile and greatest victory. When I began to hear such stories at age eighteen, they influenced me tremendously.

I got to know many Chasidic Jews from these frequent encounters.

Every Shabbat that I would visit the Rebbe, I just sat on a bench until the prayers concluded, and eventually someone would come over to me to ask the same question: "Do you have a place to eat and sleep?" I'd go with him.

Once, it was the wee hours of the morning and I wanted to go to sleep, but I just couldn't find any takers. Finally, a guy who was beardless, as I was then, said, "Come with me; I sleep in a basement with sixteen mattresses on the floor: the ultimate crash pad! I've been there three days, and nobody knows who really lives there, but it doesn't matter because they never come downstairs and we don't go upstairs." So, I went with this young guy in his twenties (who later became a professor of physics at the University of Maryland).

When I got up the next day, I crept upstairs to the living quarters of the unknown family to see whether I could get a cup of coffee. The Baumgartens were both there and treated me like a long-lost son. They wouldn't let me leave until I had at least three different pieces of cake.

I decided I was not going to waste the next three and a half years in college being depressed every day. It was either the Village or Brooklyn. The path of the Chasidim would be more difficult, so I decided to try that first, because I could always leave and hang out in the Village if things didn't work out in Brooklyn.

I took a leave of absence from YU, which I am still on, and began studying full time at the Chabad-Lubavitch Yeshiva in Newark.

Rabbi Menachem Mendel Schneerson,
the Seventh Lubavitcher Rebbe

Beatniks

Yeshiva University,
Washington Heights

CHAPTER 6

LUSTMAN FROM BALTIMORE

A week after I enrolled at the Chabad yeshiva, one of my best friends from Talmudic Academy, Mark Lustman, was gravely injured in an automobile accident and was in a coma. My new Chasidic classmates' solution? Go see the Lubavitcher Rebbe.

I was extremely upset about Lustman's accident, and I was still working out where I belonged. Basically, I gave Chabad a two-week probation. If it did it for me spiritually in two weeks, I'd stay. If not, I would go with what I was used to, hanging out in Greenwich Village.

My newfound Chabad friends said, "Tomorrow is a fabrengen. At the fabrengen, you'll ask the Rebbe for a blessing." The Rebbe presided over such gatherings on Saturday afternoons. At the fabrengen, I understood maybe every third word, because it was a three- to four-hour talk in Yiddish, but obviously there was a certain powerful magnetism there—something transcendental, something special. It was a great drug.

I'd say an hour and a half into this gathering, a line formed to the Rebbe's left, and people would come with a bottle and a little shot glass and would ask him personally for a blessing, for whatever they needed.

I said, "I don't speak Yiddish." They said, "He speaks seventy languages."

Okay, I thought, he must speak English; he's been in the United States a long time. It was three o'clock in the afternoon and I was fourth in line with my shot glass, ready to ask the Rebbe for a blessing. This would be my first time speaking to the Rebbe.

I had been in this new milieu, the Chabad world, full time for one week of my life. I was eighteen years old. Something strange began to happen when I was fourth in line to speak to the Rebbe for the first time in front of one thousand people. It was like when you have a remote for the TV, there's the volume button, and it seemed like someone had clicked the volume button down one notch when I worked my way to number three in line. When they sang, I saw their lips moving, but the sound began to recede. When I was second in line, the sound receded again. Then I was number one to go, and someone pushed the mute button, and I didn't hear any sound.

There were perhaps ten steps that separated me from the Rebbe, and I remembered what at least three or four people had told me: "Memorize what you're going to say to the Rebbe before you go to the fabrengen." My friends were *hocking* (pestering) me to remember exactly what I was planning to ask the Rebbe. It was beginning to sound like a cult; why did I have to memorize what I would say to him? My best friend, Avram Maishe ben Chana Ruchel, was in a car accident, and he's in a coma. I need a blessing for him. That's the whole message. I can remember that. Why does everybody insist that you should memorize exactly what you want to say? What was that about? No one answered that question for me. Nobody. I told other people about it and they said, "Yes, that's a good idea."

Anyway, it was my turn, so I went up to the Rebbe with my little cup of wine, and I was ambivalent: I don't know—should I tap him on the shoulder? I went up to him . . . He was listening. Nobody pushed the mute button for him. He could hear the music, the singing of one thousand people. He was waving his hand, encouraging his disciples to sing. So I figured I would begin to talk to him right next to him. He heard somebody talking to him, but he couldn't hear me because I was speaking in a regular voice, so he turned around to me and he said very loudly, "*Ah!*" Like, "What did you say?"

That "Ah!" basically erased my brain. I went blank. I forgot my friend's name. I forgot my name. I forgot what I was doing there. I'm next to the Rebbe in front of one thousand people, and I don't know why I'm there. Now it seemed like it took a long time, but it was only milliseconds before my brain went, "Oh, yes," and I started shooting out anything I remembered: "Avram Maishe ben Chana Ruchel, he's in a coma at the hospital, he's my best friend, and I need a *brachah*" (blessing)." He looked at me like he didn't understand me.

I thought for a moment, Maybe he doesn't understand English. This was becoming really difficult. Finally, he said to me, "About whom are you speaking?" In perfect English, flawless English. Heavy accent, but grammatically correct, so the good news is he understood English. The bad news is that he didn't seem to understand *me*. I just told him the whole thing. What does he mean, "About whom are you speaking?"

I didn't know what to say to that. I didn't know how to answer, so I just said again Lustman's Hebrew name, "Avram Maishe ben Chana Ruchel." The Rebbe looked down; I thought it was a couple of minutes, but it was actually a few seconds. He looked down, away from me, when I said the second time, "Avram Maishe ben Chana Ruchel." I thought maybe I didn't say it. I had a moment of doubt, but I did say my friend's name, and the Rebbe was looking down at the table, and then he popped up like, "Aha!" He didn't say "Aha!" but it was that kind of movement. Then he said, "Lustman from Baltimore."

That's talent.

When I was fifteen, somebody gave me a two-volume work, a Lubavitch rabbi's memoir. In the memoir, it said the rebbes could fly through the air doing miracles, and that everything was rosy. At the time, I thought one of two things: either they were lying, and that did not happen, or it happened one hundred years ago, when a tzaddik could do miracles, but today . . .

I mean, come on. I couldn't believe it. Somebody sitting right next to me could do miracles today?

But there it was: Lustman, the family name, and Baltimore, where he was from. That's how I knew him since before his bar mitzvah, so that's how the Rebbe related to it. I was thinking about Lustman from Baltimore, and the Rebbe pulled that out from under his yarmulke.

And it seemed to me like he said, "Listen, don't give me two weeks' probation. You're here to stay forever. You're done. Over. Bye. That's it. Are you up for it?" And I was. I knew I was going to be there indefinitely.

But there's more to this story, which I told at the forty-year reunion of my high school class. Lustman was there, and he reminded me of the part I didn't tell.

Two years later, Lustman was back in college. He was all fixed up. His bones healed, he got a new set of teeth, the whole thing, and I said to him, because Itche Springer had told me, the idea was not just to come to the Rebbe with problems and ask him for a blessing; you should thank him when things go well. I said, "Listen, Lustman, you were in a coma and you almost died. The Rebbe gave you a blessing. Now you're walking around with no residual effects and you're going to school to be a dentist like you wanted. So, come thank him."

Later that year, there was a fabrengen, and I brought Lustman. I took him over to the Rebbe in front of the whole crowd at this big gathering. I said to the Rebbe, "This is Avram Maishe ben Chana Ruchel. He was badly hurt in a car accident and you gave him a blessing, and he wants to thank you."

The Rebbe looked at him, and then looked at me, and he smiled and said, "Lustman from Baltimore." Pow. He zapped me again. He was on everybody's personal wavelength, which is more than amazing.

By the fall, after that first conversation with the Rebbe, I was studying full time, this time with no deadline. I was in.

CHAPTER 7

MY FIRST PRIVATE AUDIENCE WITH THE LUBAVITCHER REBBE

It took Schwartzie's parents a while to make their peace with their son's decision to separate from the level of Jewish observance with which he had grown up and embrace what some in the family saw as religious fanaticism. "A typical recurring argument would involve everyone in the family calling him 'Bobby' and his asking (sometimes insisting, sometimes pleading) to be called 'Shlomo' in recognition of his life choice," said nephew Ron Reisman, who as a child made many trips with his family to visit Schwartzie. "That took years to resolve."

When I was studying in Crown Heights, the Rebbe had *Yechidusin* (private audiences) Sunday, Tuesday, and Thursday night, from 8:30 or 9:30 p.m. until sometimes 5:30 in the morning. If you were a student of the yeshiva, you had the privilege of going to the Rebbe on your birthday or the Sunday, Tuesday, or Thursday nearest your birthday, to get *yechidus*, to be alone with the Rebbe.

As my birthday drew closer, I was told that on my birthday I could have a one-on-one with the Rebbe. I said, "I don't think so. I think I'd rather not." It just seemed a bit much, to be that close to someone that great. I was turning nineteen and was still somewhat ambivalent about my own religious commitment. I was thinking, "I like to read his works, to see him from a distance, but one-on-one—that's a little too intense, too heavy."

They said, "No, no. You're going to be nineteen the seventh of Kislev; you have to go in." Just as with asking for a blessing at the fabrengen, I was advised to write down what I wanted to ask. The reason is because as soon as the door closed on you and you were alone in this room with this man ... I always liken it to, when the door closes, the metal piece that clicks into the door is like a bullet shot into your heart.

This was an overwhelming experience. No one was there except the Rebbe and me, talking about ultimate, utter truth. That's scary.

You were allowed to ask one favor of the Rebbe. I was going to ask for a blessing. Then you were allowed to ask questions on Jewish law. I had heard some talk about putting on two pairs of *tefillin*.[1] For me, one was more than enough. So, I said, "I'm reluctant to ask you whether to put on Rabbeinu Tam's tefillin, because I just . . . it's so new to me."

The Rebbe didn't answer that part, so that meant, "No." Then I asked him a question on the *Tanya*, in the books of Chasidism. That one he answered.

The next year, I was a little more seasoned, but I still had been only a year and a half in the yeshiva. It was my twentieth birthday, and I went again into yechidus with the Rebbe. These *yechidusen* lasted two, maybe three minutes, not more. They were quick, because the Rebbe looked at the paper and then back at me, expressionless. His was the ultimate honesty. He didn't smile if he didn't have a reason to smile; he didn't act like a politician running for office, so he was usually expressionless. That made everything even more intense. You knew that this was a room where there had to be complete honesty and truth.

And the Rebbe said, "By your question, I see that you didn't understand what I said to you last year."

---

1   In medieval times, Rabbeinu Tam, grandson of the great Torah and Talmud commentator Rashi, began wearing a second set of tefillin containing the four verses in the Hebrew Bible that make reference to the wearing of tefillin, a practice that is maintained by some Orthodox Jews.

My first reaction was that I wanted to turn around to see whom he's talking to. Cannot be me. How many people go into this office every year? How about five years? How about ten years?

What kind of person listens that closely to something a nineteen-year-old says? That was quite powerful—that he remembered what I had said the previous year. Until then, at that point in time, I didn't really get it. I thought I got it, but I didn't really get it. Then he said my question from last year and the answer that he had given me last year, and then he added a paragraph of explanation so that I would see that my question last year was the same question I was asking this year.

It was at this juncture in my life that I became friends with Rabbi Baruch Shlomo Cunin, who would become my boss in California for the next nineteen years. He was giving a *Tanya* class at Yeshiva University. After he got married, he moved to Los Angeles as an emissary of the Lubavitcher Rebbe. I was single and didn't have summer plans. He loved my personality, and I thought he was wild and dedicated. We became very good friends when I was at YU and really hit it off. This was in 1965. He asked that I join him for the summer and travel up the coast of California to help him find Jews. We would hit phone booths, grab the Yellow Pages, and start searching for names that sounded Jewish.

The idea of "Jewish outreach" was so new and preposterous that people thought we were nuts. Even the Chasidim back in Brooklyn could not believe that we were hitting town after town looking for Jews up the California coast. I was having a great time, even though we didn't quite drive up the coast. We were more inland, going to Bakersfield, Fresno, Modesto, and so on. I remember it was 105 degrees in the shade. We slept in motels along the way. It was in Bakersfield where we experienced heavy anti-Semitism. We were looking for a motel and noticed the signs that read "Vacancy." So, Cunin and I walked in and asked the clerk at the reception for a room. The clerk told us, "We're full." This happened at a few motels in Bakersfield. I am not sure whether it was anti-Semitism, or they simply had never seen Chasidic Jews. Although in the parking lot, a few locals screamed "Smith brothers."

Either way, we were on a mission, and I was having a blast. Usually, the yeshiva gave us three weeks off in the summer. I took five weeks. I knew then that the day would come after I got married that I would also become an emissary for the Rebbe with my wife.

CHAPTER 8

OFF TO ISRAEL: MY FIRST GIG AS A RABBI

In October 1966, I left Brooklyn to study in Israel, first at a Chabad yeshiva in a newly developed village, Kfar Chabad, just outside Tel Aviv. The village had been founded in 1949 by the sixth Lubavitcher Rebbe, Joseph Isaac Schneerson, who settled it with seventy-two Russian Jewish families and put them to work as farmers. I was amazed to see Chasidic Jews operating tractors, working the fields, tending to cows, and delivering milk and the mail.

My family came to Israel for my nephew Ron's bar mitzvah that November; because Jews still lacked access to the then-Jordanian-controlled Western Wall, the ceremony took place at the Tel Aviv Sheraton.

"I have a very clear memory of him looking out the window of our room in the Tel Aviv Sheraton and seeing him register authentic shock and awe when he realized that he was looking at the Mediterranean Sea for the very first time," Reisman recalled. "He said a shehecheyanu and waxed poetic about how many times that body of water was mentioned in Talmud and how this was the first time he'd seen it with his own eyes. He was genuinely moved."

The following spring, just a couple of months before the Six-Day War, I received my first leadership assignment. The dean of the yeshiva, Efrayim Wolf, was notified that many Americans who had just made aliyah to Israel were in an absorption center in the coastal town of Netanya. There were very few Americans in the village where I was studying, so I was asked to lead a Passover seder in Netanya with another American student, Shmuel Langsam, for these American *olim chadashim*, new immigrants. We were both twenty-two years old at the time.

Fifty years later, Shmuel Langsam recounted how the evening went:

> There was a catering hall set up for the first night seder in this Netanya absorption center, with more than one hundred American immigrants. You can imagine the fear. It was six weeks before the [Six-Day] War; all Americans were ordered by the U.S. government to return home, and here you had a hundred Americans who had just migrated. They had bought one-way tickets to Israel.
>
> Schwartzie made the kiddush and started the seder. He began with, "We were once slaves in Egypt," and on that page of the Haggadah, Schwartzie explained that here the Haggadah was telling us that every woman over the age of three should light the Shabbat candles. Then, after all the participants read the next page in Hebrew, Schwartzie explained that the Haggadah is telling all boys over the age of thirteen to put on tefillin. I never saw such a thing in my life. It was wild. Schwartzie was rattling off all the mitzvot people should perform for the war effort. One man in the back of the room said to Schwartzie, "Excuse me, rabbi, I don't read Hebrew that well, but I don't see the word 'tefillin' anywhere on the page." Schwartzie responded, "I am the rabbi tonight, and I know the original Hebrew."
>
> It turned out that all the participants had a great seder with an upbeat vibe. Everybody felt more relaxed by the end of the night.

But by late May 1967, no one in Israel was relaxed. The Rebbe back in Brooklyn knew this and requested ten elder students to transfer to the yeshiva in Jerusalem called Tora Emes, which sat a few hundred feet from the Jordanian border. Nine other students and I were the chosen lucky ones.

My group of Chabad's yeshiva students sent to Israel. I'm third from the right.

CHAPTER 9

THE SIX-DAY WAR

In the spring of 1967, I was a young rabbinical student at a yeshiva in Mea She'arim, home to a large ultra-Orthodox population, just five blocks from Mandelbaum Gate, which was then a crossing point between Jordan and Israel. Israel had won its independence in 1948, but the Jordanians controlled the Old City of Jerusalem and denied Israelis access to the Western Wall, a retaining wall of the Second Temple's courtyard and a spiritual focal point of Jews worldwide.

I had to go onto the roof of a church to look through trees to see a tiny slice of the wall that Jews were not allowed to visit. The big thrill for us yeshiva boys came on Friday afternoon. No classes were held in the yeshiva, and we would go to the Mandelbaum Gate to look at the Jordanian legionnaires dressed up in their spiffy uniforms, with their guns, glaring at us.

That May, as hostile troops massed along Israel's borders, Egypt and other Arab nations imposed a blockade against Israel on the Strait of Tiran, closing the Gulf of Aqaba to Israeli vessels and ships bringing goods to Israel. Declaring the blockade an act of war and giving Egypt two weeks to lift it, the Israeli government had to determine its next step, and normal life in the Jewish state came to a tense standstill.

Panic time. Crisis time.

Because our yeshiva in Jerusalem was so close to the Jordanian border and had a lot of land, the IDF (Israel Defense Forces) took over our huge backyard, dug three huge foxholes, and put three large mortar guns inside the foxholes. We were so close to the border that you didn't have to aim.

Mortar shells could just be lobbed in the general direction of Israel or Jordan, and you were sure to hit the enemy.

The American Embassy sent a memo, then a second, and then a final notice to all American citizens in Israel. It went something like this: "War is imminent! No transportation will be provided! Leave the Country NOW!" Even my parents, who were ardent Zionists, contacted me saying that perhaps I should move to Tel Aviv because it was safer.

Orthodox Jewish-Americans in Israel had a serious moral dilemma: what to do? We Chasidim, followers of the Lubavitcher Rebbe, also weren't sure. I was an only son, born to elderly parents post-Holocaust, after they had found out that most of their siblings and their siblings' spouses and children had been murdered. Three of my four grandparents were murdered by the Nazis. I began to entertain pessimistic ideas about someone ringing my doorbell back in Atlantic City, telling my mother the bad news about her twenty-one-year-old son, killed in the most recent war in Israel.

The airport was crowded with Americans trying to escape the war, including many yeshiva students. In my yeshiva, there were four fellows from the United States. We each received a telegram from our folks. Basically, they were all identical: "Son, come home!" To get some clarity, we composed a telegram to the Lubavitcher Rebbe. We simply said, "We don't know what to do, but we are your Chasidim, so we will happily do whatever you advise."

His reply to us, in Hebrew, was short, to the point, and quite uplifting, quoting Psalm 121: "Continue studying diligently. The Guardian of Israel neither slumbers nor sleeps. We will hear good news." The daily newspaper *Ma'ariv*, looking for ways to pump up morale, printed the telegram on page one! After that, virtually no Chasidim or even Orthodox Jews left Israel.

During the two weeks of the blockade, the army moved in with thirty soldiers. Well, we were Chabad yeshiva boys, so every morning after the first study session, before we went to pray, we went out, tefillin in hands, lassoing these Israeli soldiers, pulling them in and wrapping them up to *Sh'ma yisrael*. Every morning for two weeks, we went out and we put tefillin on these guys.

The commanding officer was a man named Yossi, a tough guy. He was in charge of these thirty soldiers. The first day we put tefillin on the soldiers, Yossi the commander said, "You can't do that." We responded, "What's the problem? Take five minutes of your soldiers' time and they can go back to what they do best." What did they do for two weeks? Every day, all day, what did they do? They filled sandbags. That's all they did. Every day, all day, hundreds and hundreds of sandbags were filled because there was going to be a war. The yeshiva had dozens of windows. Sandbags were placed by the windows so the shrapnel from the mortar shells would not spray into the building.

Yossi finally negotiated a two-for-one deal. He said, "I want two yeshiva boys per soldier." One yeshiva boy filled bags of sand, and the other yeshiva boy put tefillin on the soldier. Yossi was the only one in the detachment who didn't put on tefillin.

Each Shabbat, we went out there and saw that the guys had a fire going. They were smoking, even though it was Shabbat. We went over to them with a bottle of vodka. Yossi poured everybody a *l'chaim*. These were soldiers, boys really, nineteen, twenty, twenty-one years old. They were too young. Nobody was happy there. Everybody would of course do what he had to do, but if the soldiers had their druthers, I'm sure they'd rather have been at Venice Beach.

Meanwhile, these boys were here on Shabbat. We weren't shaken by the fact that they were smoking. They weren't observant people. We brought them cake. We brought them a little *l'chaim*. One of them would say *l'chaim*, and we started singing. After a few *l'chaims*, we started dancing.

On the Sunday before the war, at about 8 a.m., a large cattle truck pulled up in front of our yeshiva and asked for volunteers for noncombat work. I, along with another thirty from the yeshiva student body, got into that dirty cattle truck with absolutely no idea as to where we were going or what we were supposed to do.

But, being Chasidim, we trusted in the Rebbe's blessings and even became enthusiastic about the war effort. It turned out that there was some new housing that did not have a shelter. But the houses were right on the border, next to a huge open field that led to Jordan. There was nobody there; it was the end of the city. Jordan was right there.

We were informed that it was our job to dig trenches for the people living in the new apartments. I learned something.

Before you dig trenches, you need to remove the larger rocks in the field. But nobody gave us gloves. After a few hours, all our hands were bleeding. There was one soldier with a pistol and thirty of us Torah scholars. By noon, the trenches were about knee deep. Everybody, the Americans at least, had bleeding hands. I told the soldier with us, "My hand's bleeding." He said, "OK." He meant, "Continue. You're a yeshiva boy, a creampuff

American boy; now get your hands dirty again. You came finally for one morning."

We continued. By 11:30, I saw that the binoculars, this soldier's army binoculars, were being passed from one yeshiva boy to the next. People were standing on this side of our trench. Everybody was looking toward the deserted houses right beyond the No Man's Land. I stood in line, got the binoculars, and looked through them. I saw that on the roof of the deserted building were Jordanian soldiers looking right at us with binoculars. I told the officer, "I think it's time to go for lunch."

About ten minutes later, for the very first time in my life, I heard and experienced the sound of machine gun fire directed at me. All of us jumped into the freshly dug trenches. I again started entertaining some pessimistic thoughts. We were thirty guys and one pistol. Those people across the field could just walk the two blocks and go, "bang, bang, bang," and take out all the yeshiva boys.

As a kid, when I went to the movies and saw cops and robbers, I'd hear a machine gun and find it kind of cool. It was exciting. But when you hear it live and it's aimed at you, it sounds like a death rattle. It's ugly. There's a certain obscenity to it. It's incredibly impersonal. Whoever's doing that wants to kill people he doesn't even know.

We dove into this trench, and we essentially had our noses shoved into this little hole that we had dug. Every once in a while, people lifted up their heads to see what was occurring; the bullets were close. They went over the trench and in front of the trench. When they hit the ground, they made a spray.

I hated not being active at a time like that. So I started singing an uplifting, happy Chasidic melody. Immediately the rest of the students joined me.

Our commanding officer went ballistic.

I don't really know what he screamed at us in Hebrew. But I responded that the Jordanian soldiers knew our position, so what difference did it make? To tell the truth, we were so far away from the main part of the city, on the desolate outskirts, that we weren't sure that anyone knew we were alive or that we were being fired upon.

Thank G-d, after ten minutes, we heard returning fire from Israelis. After another ten minutes, it grew quiet. Jeeps came from the Israeli side and they parked the equivalent of half a block away on the field. Soldiers with machine guns were mounted on the jeeps. They got down on the ground and crawled over to our position. Each yeshiva boy went back crawling with these guys to where the jeeps were parked, but no one was shot while crawling. That was the first time I really heard a machine gun fired. That was one day before the war began.

The Civil Defense of Israel had commandeered our entire yeshiva building because it was large, and we were only a few minutes' walking distance from the Mandelbaum Gate. Every night, there had to be one yeshiva boy sitting in the office the whole night, in case the phone rang. That Sunday night, the night before the war started, was my night. Nobody ever told you what to do should the phone ring.

It was about 3 a.m. I was reading a book and babysitting the phone. Three in the morning in Jerusalem means it was dead silent. So, I was reading this book, and suddenly I thought, "You know, that's funny. I'm imagining that the phone is ringing." Then I imagined it again. I thought, "I don't believe this: on my watch, the phone has to ring."

I thought, "What happens if I don't pick up the phone? Does that mean there's not going to be a war? Maybe I won't pick up the phone." Anyway, I kind of felt that I had no choice and answered the phone. The operator on the line said, "Hello, we have a person-to-person call for Shlomo Schwartz from Atlantic City, New Jersey." I could barely get out the single word, "Speaking."

It was my parents, my nephew, and my two sisters. That was my entire family. They were calling, wanting to find out how I was.

My father asked me, "How is it there?"

I said, "Everything's fine; it's all exaggerated in the newspaper. Everything's going to be fine."

He said, "Do you know that Jerusalem's surrounded on three sides by Jordan? Why don't you go to Tel Aviv?"

I told them everything was really just fine. It was a great call, and I felt terrific about reassuring my family.

A few hours later, as we had been every morning for the last two weeks, we were in the yeshiva courtyard, hanging out with our new friends, putting on tefillin with the young soldiers.

* * *

About 8:15 in the morning, the machine gun fire started. OK, here we go again. We crawled like snakes, like dogs, across the courtyard back into the yeshiva. The soldiers and the students crawled into the yeshiva. We didn't know until the radio told us that this was the beginning of the war.

We went inside the building with the dormitories, where there was a bunch of beds. People ran in from the street. The building should hold about twenty, but now forty people ran in from here and there. There was machine gun fire for about two hours. The truth is, though, that nobody was scared because we were in that hundred-year-old Mea She'arim building. The stone walls were *thick*. Machine gun fire was not a problem. People were sitting on the floor. We didn't turn off the lights. We had all the sandbags in the windows—many, many sandbags.

Two hours later, the bombardment of mortar fire began. Things changed radically. Mortar fire is real war. It's very different. The Jordanians were indiscriminately lobbing thousands of these mortars, three or four blocks from where we were. For maybe eight hours, every three minutes, we heard the following sounds: the first time there was an explosion, it got quiet in the room. Then, pretty much every three, four minutes, we heard "sssss." Then it was quiet for three seconds. That was the most terrifying time because after those three seconds were up, an explosion would occur. The question was, would you be alive afterward?

Every three minutes, this was . . . the noise was so loud, so terrifying that we had to make peace with not seeing our families. It's like the thing that happens just before an accident—your whole life flashes before your eyes. That happened something like every three minutes. It was unnerving. Two people among the forty went insane. An eighteen-year-old boy was very red in the face and fell down and started crying. A forty-two-year-old man started crying that eight blocks away were his wife and his children. The explosions, the bombs—he didn't know whether they were alive or dead.

Among the forty people, we had one soldier, a sergeant, with a pistol. He just walked over to this forty-two-year-old man, blubbering and talking about his children, and the soldier hauled off and whammed the man across the face. The guy just continued crying quietly, but people definitely would have flipped out because of him. The ugliness of war is pretty apparent when you're in it. This continued. Then it looked like somebody told the Jordanians that there were three foxholes in our courtyard, four blocks away, and they should take them out.

They started dropping shells every three minutes. I could hear it when it was far away and then hear it grow a little closer, a little closer. For perhaps three hours, it was intense. One mortar, instead of wiping out the foxholes, fell short and onto our building. There was a car parked in front of the door of the building. The mortar shell hit the car, and the car exploded. It was quiet for a long time in our room. You really didn't know whether you were alive or not. It was that kind of explosion. This was a constant, minute-by-minute situation that dragged on.

This happened Monday, perhaps at 10:30 in the morning until the middle of the night. Around 3 a.m., there was a lull in the mortar bombardment. We also, in that time, took a hit in the roof from two shells, which made a hole. Another two made a hole in the ceiling in the room we were in. You could see the sky and the stars. We could see that the sky was pink from the explosions of the bombardment, like a light show. At one point, when it was raining down on us, the IDF took a direct hit and two guys were killed, two soldiers.

The Jordanians pretty much wiped out that emplacement. That's how bad it was around where we were. I was under a bed with the sergeant. I was hoping the shrapnel would not go through the bed. Around three or four in the morning, we heard a noise. A different kind of noise. A noise that was getting closer. I didn't know whether this was good news or bad. The noise grew louder, and we realized that the noise was a tank. The problem was, we were so close to the border that we didn't know whether it was our tank or theirs.

The first thing that everybody said was, "Don't go underneath the beds," because the tank shell could do a lot of damage in our little dormitory room. We didn't have a shelter. After that, a few people decided to peek through the sandbags to see whose tank it was. If it's a Jordanian tank, that's not good news. If it's an Israeli tank going toward No Man's Land, that means we're progressing; we're going toward the Old City.

At this point, everybody jumped onto the sandbags and looked through. As the tank was passing by our window, we saw a white sign and a blue Jewish star. It was an Israeli tank, and we started cheering. This is what we were waiting for the whole time.

We listened hour after hour to the radio reports. They were talking about everything but Jerusalem. Yossi, the commanding officer, came in with a fifty-pound note. He said he wanted to donate it for a new *ner tamid*, a perpetual light, and it should have two names on it, the two soldiers who had been killed.

By Wednesday, all the explosions we heard were in the far distance. We barely heard the action. It was June in the Middle East, the sun was shining, and it was a warm, beautiful day. Gradually, we floated outside onto the quiet, deserted street. It certainly seemed that the war was moving away from our neighborhood, so it was kind of over for us (or so we thought). It did seem a bit unrealistic, but after being incarcerated for almost seventy-two hours and having survived a never-to-be-forgotten bombardment that lasted an extremely motivational four hours, it was a deep pleasure just to stand outside in the quietude of the glorious, blue Israeli sky and to be nearly coerced to elevate into deeper themes of mortality, spirituality, the meaning of life, personal goals, and so forth.

Suddenly an army jeep with soldiers screeched up to us, and the officer shouted, "We need volunteers!" Eight blocks away, there were two shelters overcrowded with civilian women and children. The men were all at the battlefronts, and the little children and women had no food. "We have bags of fresh bread and bottles of milk," the soldiers said. "Get in the jeeps, and we'll drop you there with the milk and bread. You will distribute the food, and then you will make a temporary toilet for the adults."

I cannot tell you how we were welcomed by the panic-stricken, crying women and children.

* * *

At 10 p.m. Wednesday night, right where we were, the bombardment started again. The sound of twenty or thirty adult women and fifty kids screaming hysterically was so horrific that I decided I'd rather go out there. I understood the screaming. This explosion hits and, basically, you think you're going to die. But these people were screaming their guts out. I wasn't staying for that. I couldn't take the screaming.

As I stood in the doorway of the shelter planning my route back to the yeshiva, I saw a miracle. One of the mortar shells had hit a roof on the second story of a dwelling and had started a fire. It was one of a bunch of little houses crowded together, connected. The whole block could have gone up. But in Israel, every roof had something called a *dud shemesh*, a big barrel full of water, which provided hot water through solar heating. The next shell that hit the same spot exploded into shrapnel, and the shrapnel hit the rain barrel and caused a shower, which put out the fire. I read this in the Jewish press a couple of weeks later. Ordinarily, I would say, "Come on." But I saw it.

It was 11:30 at night. There was tremendous bombardment, explosions, mortar fire. It was light as day, and the whole sky was pink, with tracers going through. A tremendous light show.

Any one of these things could end your life or maim you, especially if you see the shrapnel near you. I remember thinking, *I'm an only son. My poor mother—I'm not going to tell her this story. I'm not going to get to tell her this story.* Then I thought, *OK, listen, let the good Lord have mercy.* Bashert *(preordained) is* bashert; *if it's supposed to be me, then I'll get it where I'm going to get it.* I was just going to run the eight blocks back to the yeshiva.

I ran, and I made it. I got to the yeshiva. The first thing Yossi said to me was, "Where are the other guys?" They all came back three hours later.

CHAPTER 10

THE WESTERN WALL

Remember that from 1948 to 1967, no Jews were allowed near the *Kotel* (Western Wall). And in the days immediately after the Israelis took back the Old City, on June 7, the IDF wouldn't allow the civilian population to go to the Kotel either, because the Arabs had strewn the paths to the Kotel with anti-personnel mines. The Jordanians were clearly aware that after they had deprived the Jews of visiting their most hallowed place for nineteen years, there would be a rush of our people to the Kotel. Imagine if Israel had not allowed Muslims to visit Mecca as the spoils of a war!

I saw some people going along the shortcuts known by those who had lived in the Old City before 1948. Those shortcuts bypassed the soldiers, who would have stopped these people. Many of them came back without legs. Anti-personnel mines aren't designed to kill you; they're meant to maim and tear off limbs so that the victim will be a burden to society forever. An elderly man I knew led a group to the Kotel and came back in a wheelchair because he had his leg blown off. A father brought his eight-year-old daughter with him to kiss the Kotel. Shortly thereafter, he was trying to get her fitted for a prosthetic leg.

I decided that if Almighty G-d saved me from the bombardment, I could wait until it was safe to go to the Kotel. I wasn't in a rush. I didn't need to be a *nudnik* to the Almighty to make some more miracles just to save my *tuchis*.

The following week brought the first night of Shavuot, and we had been studying all night at the yeshiva. At 4:30 a.m., we were thinking about going to the *mikvah* (ritual bath) before praying the morning service. We became aware of a strange noise that was coming from Mea She'arim Street and growing louder and louder. We looked out the window and then went outside. It was people. There were thousands of people, walking quickly but in an orderly way, completely filling the ancient, narrow street. Their shoes shuffling on the cobblestones made the strange noise. We looked at the first Jew who made eye contact, and he said, "The army cleaned up a longer but safe way to the Western Wall."

We all ran to the mikvah and then became part of what appeared to be a river of thousands of people. As it started to get light outside, silhouettes on the roofs of all the houses could be seen: Israeli soldiers holding machine guns, guarding us. But as the light increased, we were even more impressed by the ever-growing crowd. The excitement was palpable, though almost no one talked. It was spontaneous: a group unity with a singleness of purpose!

By the time we got to the Kotel, there were already two rows of people spreading across it. The sun hadn't fully risen, but the Jews were wailing away; they were praying their hearts out! It was moving to watch and to just be there to observe it all. All the while, hundreds of people continued streaming in. As each group arrived, it started its own service. It was a cacophony, but there was nothing ugly about the sound being made. The amalgam of the different melodies of the heart-wrenching, devotional, sincere prayers for the holiday was uplifting, all blessings pointed in the same direction.

We prayed up a storm for about four hours and then headed back to our dorm. When we turned around from the Kotel, we saw that the crowd of worshipers had become nine deep, and the river of humanity flowing into the plaza had grown to about five times its former width. After all, it was the first Shavuot the Jews were permitted to be at their holiest site in nineteen years.

What a Shavuot holiday!

Envelope of letter from the Rebbe sent May 23, 1967, less than two weeks before the Six-Day War began

Letter from the Rebbe addressed to Schwartzie and his 3 friends

IDF soldiers clearing a plaza by the Western Wall, 1967

IDF soldiers resting at the Western Wall, 1967

ELEVEN-MONTH ENGAGEMENT

I returned to the United States not long after the Six-Day War. That summer, I met the young woman who would become my first wife, Alta Shula Deitsch, from a Chasidic Crown Heights family. My family had largely made peace with my affiliation with Chabad, but my father, who had retired as cantor of Chelsea Hebrew Congregation, was still concerned about my prospects. My sister Greta summarized the family's attitude toward my developing career in Chabad and my impending marriage:

After the Six-Day War, my brother Bobby was seeing old school friends in New York, and the father of one friend invited him for dinner. That's where he met his first wife, Alta. After a few dates, he informed his parents of his intention to become engaged and invited them to meet his prospective bride and her family.

My father was shocked, but he was also a little pleased. His son would not be alone; he would share his life with someone and have a partner in life. Papa's approaching old age worried him,

and he wanted to see his son settled. I worried about meeting my new sister-in-law-to-be, since my father thought my brother truly deserved Miss America, but was not yet ready to take on the responsibility of a wife, as he had no income to support even himself. He was merely a twenty-two-year-old student, and my father did not believe in putting the cart before the horse.

However, the Lubavitcher philosophy disagreed with ours, and, according to my sister-in-law's father, a couple

> married first and only later worried about living expenses. After having struggled a lifetime to support his family, my father found this kind of wisdom strange and impractical. But though he had misgivings, he openly accepted my brother's choice. There was no point in arguing, since my brother really asked no one's advice anyhow and had already made his choice, whether his family approved or disapproved. He had chosen to become a Lubavitcher and had decided to follow their lifestyle and reject the [material] values of his own family. Or at least he gave that impression. Because we loved him, we wished him well and buried our doubts so as not to alienate him.

To make matters even more complicated between our two families, the Rebbe sent me back to Israel for another eleven months. I almost missed my own engagement party. This is what happened:

Looking forward to getting married, I wrote to the Rebbe about my engagement following the High Holidays and my plans of studying in Newark, New Jersey, which was close by, in preparation for the wedding.

The Rebbe didn't answer. (Very uncommon, especially at that time.) So I wrote to him again with a full list of the reasons I would benefit from studying in Newark; for example, I would be learning with the eminent Rabbi Izzy Friedman, along with a slew of able *chavrusas* (study partners).

At the end of this letter, I also mentioned that if the Rebbe wanted me to study in Israel for another year, I would do so. My name was already on a list compiled for a *kevutza* (a group of yeshiva students) to be sent to the Toras Emes Yeshiva in Jerusalem.

The Rebbe replied, *Nachon l'hachzir, ulipeleh hasofek,* "It would be proper to return and a wonder of your doubt."

The following day, I heard that the Rebbe's chief secretary, Rabbi Hadikov, was looking for me. I then heard that Rabbi Binyomin Klein was looking for me. The buzz was all over Crown Heights. When I entered Hadikov's office, he told me, "You don't have a visa to stay in this country. The Rebbe said to go to Israel, and that means now." I told Hadikov that my engagement party was set for five days from then and that my fiancée and her parents would not be pleased to have a party without my being there. Rabbi Hadikov then said, "If you can make a *shaliach* to *mikadesh* somebody for *nisuin*, then you can make a *shaliach* for an engagement."

(In other words, the Rabbi was telling me I need not be present for my own engagement party.)

Hadikov then said that I should get a plane ticket and go to Israel. I replied, "I don't have $300, which is the cost of a plane ticket." As my parents were not pleased of my entry into Chabad in the first place, I was unable to ask them for what was a large sum of money in those days. Never mind that I was supposed to be married in a few months. So with no choice, I requested Rabbi Hadikov to supply the money. Rabbi Hadikov said, "I will not give you the money, as this is not my issue."

I then had the task of breaking the news to my future father-in-law, Sholom Deitsch, that I was not going to make the engagement party, as the Rebbe had requested that I return to Israel immediately. Sholom asked me whether the Rebbe said to go now, or was it Hadikov? I said, "I don't know," thinking, here I am, an innocent boy from Atlantic City marrying into a prestigious Chabad family, and I'm getting caught in a tumultuous cross-fire.

My father-in-law, who had access to the Rebbe and his secretaries, dragged me to Chabad headquarters in Brooklyn and first went into Hadikov's office. I was outside the office and heard Sholom screaming, "Was this you, or did the Rebbe say so?" Hadikov said, "This is my interpretation as to what should be done." Sholom then said, "He will stay until after the engagement party," and left the office with me in tow.

I now realized that I needed $300, and dared to ask my future infuriated father-in-law, who had to break the news to the mother of the bride that the groom would be leaving the country in a few days. I then went downstairs to the sanctuary in 770 and told everybody the story and put my hand out to collect the money. Within twenty minutes, I had the $300.

After the engagement party, the Deitsch family, including me, went into yechidus for a private audience with the Rebbe. Sholom told the Rebbe that the family had to make wedding arrangements, and that we needed a wedding date. (This was an uncommon procedure, as the family would typically present the Rebbe with possible dates, and the Rebbe would choose one.) Here, however, Sholom didn't present possible dates because he had no idea when I would be able to return from Israel. By Sholom asking the Rebbe for a wedding date, he was really asking when his future son-in-law could return from Israel. The Rebbe looked at Sholom and waited for a date to be presented. Sholom then asked whether Shavuot would be a good time. (This was seven months down the road). The Rebbe smiled and said that the *chassan* (groom) would not be home then. Sholom then asked, how about the twelfth of Tammuz? (This was nine months later.) The Rebbe said the chassan would still not have returned. Sholom then asked for *Rosh Chodesh* Elul (eleven months from the meeting date), to which the Rebbe said, "That would be a great time."

And that's how my engagement lasted eleven months.

CHAPTER 12

MARRIAGE AND FAMILY DYNAMICS

I married Alta upon my return to New York from my second stint in Israel, in the summer of 1968. The plan was for me to spend another year at Chabad headquarters in Crown Heights and then become a Chabad emissary in California. I had been married only a couple of months when Alta's father, Sholom, died at age fifty-one. I really wanted to head out to California, but my wife had just lost her father. It was a huge tragedy in Lubavitch—Sholom's wife was left a widow with six kids.

At that time, we were living in a small apartment in Crown Heights. My mother-in-law, Mirel, had an empty apartment under her own. So she said to my wife and me, "Move underneath me. I live in a duplex. I own it. It's rent-free. I'm on top. You're in the bottom." And I said, "I don't want to do that."

It was customary that when a woman was pregnant, she would go with her husband for a yechidus with the Rebbe in her fifth month and her ninth month. So, the family suggested that we ask the Rebbe whether we should move in under Alta's mother.

I said, "I don't want to ask that question, because I don't have a question." If I had a question, for me the answer was no.

They came back with, "It's not a question for you, but it is a question for Alta." OK, family pressure. Finally, I communicated to the Rebbe, "I'm reluctant to ask this question, because I don't want to do it, but the family, including my wife, is pressuring me to move into the apartment underneath my *shviger* (mother-in-law) rent-free. Everything would be rosy, but I feel it's too close for comfort."

The Rebbe said, "To live in the same neighborhood is not bad, but sometimes too close is not healthy; not for her, not for you." In other words, be in Crown Heights, but being in that apartment was not the way to go.

My mother-in-law backed off immediately. There was no argument, no explanation needed. She was definitely a Chasid of the Rebbe. Whatever had been said, boom, it was over in a second, even though she had pushed very strongly for us to move in there.

It proved an interesting lesson in family dynamics and communication. She did in fact have a good point. She was a young widow, so why shouldn't I move in? It would help her out, having her daughter right there. She would have a place to go and could see (future) grandchildren. The Rebbe stopped that. He was also thinking about the future side of the equation, the fact that we were leaving Brooklyn in less than a year to go to California. We needed to consider that, even though the whole family was on one side. I certainly appreciated the Rebbe's position.

Just prior to my father-in-law's passing, his oldest son, Zalman, got engaged. Sholom said to the Rebbe during a fabrengen, "I want to thank the Rebbe for the match" (between his son Zalman and his bride Tzirel). The Rebbe responded, "If I'm the matchmaker, then you owe me for the matchmaker's fee." This was a big deal, actually, because the Rebbe was not the matchmaker. But Sholom, whom I looked up to like a father, was a major and devout disciple of the Rebbe. To show his commitment and deep connection to the Rebbe, he claimed that the Rebbe was the true matchmaker. And the Rebbe accepted this notion.

Following the fabrengen, Sholom went home excitedly and told his wife about the conversation with the Rebbe. They were trying to figure out what the Rebbe would want from them. As Sholom was clean-shaven, they thought perhaps the Rebbe would ask him to grow a beard. They never found out because just a little while later, Sholom passed away. My mother-in-law was upset that the Rebbe had requested a matchmaker's fee from her husband and that he never found out what it entailed.

Once, when my wife and I were in a yechidus with the Rebbe, he said to us, "You should fix it so that the widow, your mother-in-law, Alta's mother, should come see me for yechidus." We tried and failed. She said, "Why? Is it going to bring Sholom back? He's dead. It's over."

Prior to Zalman's wedding, the entire Deitsch family, myself included, went into yechidus. I knew this was going to be a showdown between Mirel, the new widow, and the Rebbe. Many things happened in this yechidus. I didn't say a word. I watched and listened. Every time Mirel cried about her husband's death, the Rebbe immediately stopped speaking and waited for her to finish. This happened four times.

Mirel asked the Rebbe, "How will I not ruin the wedding if I cry at the wedding?" And the Rebbe responded, "That's right, if you cry under the *chuppah* (wedding canopy), you will ruin the wedding." I couldn't believe it; the Rebbe was telling the recently widowed woman that she could not cry at her son's wedding. At Zalman's wedding, I made sure to stand in such a way as to view my mother in-law throughout the entire ceremony to see whether she cried. I saw her biting her lips the entire time, but she didn't cry.

In that same yechidus with the Rebbe, Mirel brought up the matchmaker's fee that the Rebbe had requested from her husband. Mirel said, "Since my husband is no longer here to give you this matchmaker's fee, maybe the Rebbe would like to ask it from me?"

And the Rebbe responded, "In a previous yechidus, your husband Sholom told me, 'I feel like I'm sitting on a bomb that's about to explode.'" (He'd had a number of heart attacks over the past three years.) And the Rebbe continued, "I told your husband, 'You're sitting in G-d's hands.'"

So, when Mirel asked what the Rebbe wanted for a matchmaking fee, the Rebbe said, "I was going to ask from your husband a strengthening of his faith in G-d, to trust in confidence that he was going to be healthy and well, because that's the vessel into which falls G-d's blessing of health. And since your husband is not here, I will ask you to have this faith and trust."

There was another time the Rebbe talked to me about trust in G-d: when our first child, Chanele, was born. The umbilical cord had been wrapped around her neck three times, cutting off her air supply, so she was born blind and with severe cognitive disabilities. Obviously, we knew it was a trauma, but in 1969, you couldn't determine whether a baby could see until six weeks after birth. It would take much longer to find out about the mental/intellectual issues.

I asked the Rebbe, "What should I pray for? Should I pray for a miracle? Or should I acknowledge that it is what it is, so give me the strength to receive what it is? What does trust in G-d mean? Trust that G-d will make a miracle, or trust that you're going to get less than you deserve?" (The doctors didn't give her much time to live.)

The Rebbe answered, "We have to have trust in G-d that things can right themselves, even if there is no miracle, because, daily, they're finding new treatments in every facet of medicine, so you can pray that they find it faster, whatever it is." Trust in G-d, he was saying—that's the vessel in which these blessings I give you can form and materialize.

Almost fifty years later, Chanele is still living.

My engagement party. Left to right: Mottel Deitsch, brother-in-law Cy Tabak, my father, nephew Ron Reisman, me, my father in-law Sholom Deitsch, Mendel Futerfas's brother Hendel Lieberman, Dovid Deitsch in gray hat

CHAPTER 13

BLOOD TRANSFUSION

I lost my own father, Cantor Morris Schwartz, in the spring of 1969, about six months after Alta's father died. He had been ill for a long time. One year prior, on a Shabbat afternoon in winter, the phone started ringing, ten times and stopping, ten times and stopping, and continued to do that for about an hour, so, obviously, someone was trying to get in touch with me, but I wasn't answering the phone because it was Shabbat. Then, two hours later, the doorbell rang. It was a telegram: your father's in a coma. Deathly ill. Come immediately to Atlantic City Hospital.

There was half an hour left until Shabbat was over. I went to 770 and told Rabbi Leibel Groner, the Rebbe's secretary, that my father was deathly ill and I wanted to get a blessing from the Rebbe before traveling to Atlantic City.

The trip by car took two and a half hours, so Leibel said, "OK, this is what we'll do. During *ma'ariv* (the evening service), you're going to hide under the stairs in the waiting room to the Rebbe's office. When the Rebbe returns from *ma'ariv* into the waiting room, I'm going to close the door." That door was always open on Saturday evening because the *bocherim*, the yeshiva boys, would want to talk to the Rebbe until the last second. "After I close the door, you'll come out from under the stairs in the waiting room," Leibel said. "You'll go to the Rebbe and ask him for a *brachah* (blessing), and then you'll go to Atlantic City."

As soon as he closed the door, the yeshiva students started pushing it. They didn't want the door to be closed. They wanted to see the Rebbe until the last second, but Leibel closed the door, and the Rebbe looked at the door being closed, because that wasn't typical. Then I approached him, and he realized it was a setup. I told him, "My father is in a coma, and I got a telegram that he is deathly ill. I need a *brachah* for Moishe ben Rivka."

The Rebbe looked at me very strongly, matching my desperate stare, and said, "Schwartz from Atlantic City." Although I'd been around for a while, I didn't think he really knew me, because I was just another yeshiva boy. He asked, "What does he have? What's wrong with him?"

I really didn't want to have a medical conversation. I didn't even like being one on one in closed quarters with him. Just give me a *brachah* and let me go. I didn't say that, but I wanted out. It was nerve-racking. My father was dying. I said, "He has leukemia."

Then the Rebbe asked, "Has he had a transfusion?" He said it as though he was a consulting doctor on the case. Then he said, "Your father should have a *refuah m'hirah*," a speedy recovery. Now the usual language is *refuah shlemah*, a complete recovery. Well, back then, you couldn't get *refuah shlemah* with leukemia. Leukemia was incurable, so he said "a speedy recovery." That was the Rebbe—these nuances, these subtleties.

Before I drove to Atlantic City, I called my family in the hospital and requested that the doctors perform a blood transfusion immediately. The chief doctor got on the phone and requested that I first come to the hospital before I dictate medical procedures for his patient. I said, "There is a blood specialist in New York and he requested a blood transfusion be done on the patient." The doctor responded, "You mean there is a blood specialist who has not seen the patient and is giving out recommendations?" I couldn't convince the doctor.

At any rate, when I got to the hospital, my father was already out of the coma, and when I told him about my conversation with the Rebbe, he said, "You're missing the Rebbe's fabrengen." He had the presence of mind, even being perhaps only two hours out of the coma, to put this together, even though he had never been at a fabrengen. He knew where he was in the present moment, and he put it together that way. The next day, an ambulance took him to Philadelphia, and the first thing the hematologist said was that my father needed a transfusion.

* * *

Another of the Rebbe's higher mental powers I witnessed occurred at a public fabrengen during the week.

There was this professor of math at Columbia who had become a *ba'al teshuvah* (newly observant) with a beard, the coat to his knees, the whole thing. He didn't understand Yiddish, but he came to fabrengen a couple of times a year.

One day, the Rebbe was speaking. The professor didn't understand a word, so he started writing down a mathematical formula on the paper tablecloth. He was sitting very far away from the Rebbe, but the Rebbe saw what the professor was doing out of the corner of his eye and said, toward the end of the fabrengen, "I want to see that."

The professor hesitated. I think somebody jumped at the tablecloth and ripped the whole thing out and brought it right to the Rebbe. He looked at the formula, like eight lines of numbers, and he went to the second or third line and said, "Here's the mistake," and the professor lost his marbles. He was already a Chasid, but he looked at the Rebbe like, "You have to be kidding." The Rebbe was right—there was an error in the formula.

It was just an aside, but everybody at that fabrengen saw it. I was there.

Life in Crown Heights with the Rebbe was truly magical.

CAMPUS RABBI

CHAPTER 14

FIRST CHABAD CAMPUS RABBI ON PLANET EARTH

I was in no hurry to leave the Holy Land—Brooklyn, that is. I had been to California once before, during the summer of '65, as a sort of student intern to assist Rabbi Baruch Shlomo Cunin, Chabad's first emissary to the West Coast, who had moved there the previous year. Cunin wrote to the Rebbe after I got married, requesting that I become an emissary in California. The Rebbe didn't answer. After my father in-law, Sholom, died a few months later, we understood why the Rebbe had not granted permission for Alta and me to travel. So, Cunin wrote a second time to the Rebbe after the *shiva* (seven-day mourning period). Again, the Rebbe didn't respond. After my father, Morris, passed away a few months later, we understood again why the Rebbe had not granted us permission. The Rebbe had felt that we should stay put to help our families.

Cunin finally landed me on the third try. He said he wanted me for UCLA to start the planet's first Chabad on a university campus. He needed an answer by Sunday. This was on Thursday night. The Rebbe then told me to seek advice from Rabbi Shmuel Dovid Raichik, who had been living in Los Angeles since 1949 under the directive of the previous Lubavitch Rebbe. After getting the clearance from all parties, including my wife, we were off to the golden coast of California.

> *"Shlomo really made the model for the Chabad House on campus,"* Olivia said. *"UCLA's was the first. Chabad had had synagogues that were community-based, but there was never anything on a campus before 1969. Shlomo came out with Rabbi Cunin and they created this model."* Schwartzie was also instrumental in opening Chabad campus centers at two other University of California campuses: the flagship campus, UC Berkeley, and UC San Diego in La Jolla. It was Schwartzie, Olivia said, who came up with *"what you do on campus: how you approach people, what you say, what classes you teach, how you interact, all that."*

I came to California during an era of tremendous upheaval among young Jews that had started when the baby-boom generation began to come of age in the mid-sixties. Part of the cultural rebellion among Jewish college students of that era involved experimentation with religious movements other than those in which they'd been raised: it was when you would hear an undergraduate, when asked whether he or she were Jewish, respond with, "Well, my parents are." Eastern philosophies and rituals attracted thousands of Jews.

At the same time, there was a spike in the proportion of Jews who were marrying non-Jews. The taboo against marrying non-Jews among non-Orthodox Jews shattered; what had been a 10-percent rate of intermarriage in the early sixties was estimated at 33 percent by 1973. By 2000, it was 49 percent. In 2013, it was 72 percent, based on the Pew Research study of that year, and 85 percent based on a 2016 analysis of the Pew study by Rabbi Antony Gordon and Richard M. Horowitz of the Orthodox organization Aish ha-Torah.

It was clear then, and it's clear now: where we win or lose is on the college campus. Opening a Chabad House also dovetailed with my mandate as a Lubavitcher.

> *"It was more a function of Jewish survival and winning the war of assimilation at all costs, and with any tactic that would work,"* said Schwartzie's son-in-law Jacob. *"He needed to find a way to connect to Jews who were not interested, so whatever it took to achieve that end, as a soldier of the Rebbe, that was his mission."*

The struggle to win Jewish hearts and minds, Schwartzie told his son Mayshe, could be brutal. "No one was interested in Judaism, let alone Orthodox Judaism," Mayshe said. "Every day,

they would wake up and fight against every enticing attraction and exciting cause they competed with. And they were losing."

There were propitious factors, though, for Chabad during the seventies. There was always tremendous dialogue on campus. There was openness; people were open to ideas, open to each other. There were a great many psychology majors and philosophy majors, and not so many business majors. People were open to communicating different ideas without feeling that they had to kill the person sitting in front of them. And, in terms of being able to share Judaism, too, people were open.

The seventies also saw the first blossoming of the ba'al teshuvah phenomenon: Jews who had grown up without Jewish education, or who had come through what they saw as a sterile, unspiritual experience in synagogues, embraced Orthodoxy as a more authentic and meaningful form of Judaism. UCLA Chabad House was open to the entire Jewish community, not just students, and many Jewish spiritual seekers walked through its doors. There was nothing for nonreligious Jews anywhere else in Los Angeles. The Passover seders that we made in the Chabad House had at times 700 people in attendance. There was no one else doing something on that level—doing outreach to completely unaffiliated Jews who weren't going to Reform synagogues and weren't going to Conservative synagogues and were just falling by the wayside.

Still, connecting on campus was a challenge, and I knew the black suit, white dress shirt, and black hat constituted a barrier between me and many of the long-haired, tie-dyed students. It wasn't long before I swapped my black pants for blue jeans and started my collection of T-shirts. You can't be intimidating to college kids if you're wearing rainbow suspenders and a T-shirt reading, "I Survived Hebrew School." The college kids stopped calling me Rabbi Schwartz and adopted the name "Schwartzie."

"He loved his jeans," Olivia said. "Often, in the early years that he was working, he was threatened to be fired for the way he dressed. He never backed down. He has the most amazing T-shirt collection with sayings from everywhere in the world and every place we had ever been. One of those things we talked about was his colorful rainbow suspenders and why he wore them. Because you couldn't say no if he asked you to shake a lulav when he was wearing those suspenders; it would be very hard for you to turn him down."

Moshe Parry first encountered Schwartzie as a brand-new freshman:

September 1973 . . . UCLA . . . Bruin Walk . . . Coming down the hill minding my own business. I stop near the bottom as a crowd of people are gathered around someone I cannot as yet see. When I approach, a spot opens so I can be part of the circle. I'm there in my cut-off blue jeans, purple Neil Young T-shirt and brown leather sandals, my long Jewfro-shag flying behind and on top of me like a mane on a lion, and I have a full, long beard, but not as long as the beard on the man I encounter.

I come face to face with a rabbi who greets me as if we've known each other all our lives. He is wearing a very long, colorful tie-dyed T-shirt with blue jeans held up by red suspenders, and he has a large yarmulke perched upon the top of his head—Yemenite, I seem to remember. But all of this pales into insignificance when I notice that he is literally covered from head to toe with buttons and ribbons and banners: Ask me why I'm Jewish . . . Torah this and Torah that . . . I love Israel . . . and so on, and so on. He's a walking billboard for all things Jewish. I start to laugh; he's a Jewboard! What in heaven's name is this grown man doing?

We all know now exactly what Schwartzie was doing: he was playing the jester l'shem shamayim, in heaven's name . . . he was engaging in kiruv, ingathering. To save Jewish souls and bring them back to Torah-true Judaism, he was willing to get all dressed up in a ridiculous outfit so we would smile. Then the ice would be broken and he could invite us in for Shabbat or to learn some Torah.

How many of us out there owe our first real encounter with Torah Judaism as an adult to Schwartzie's kiruv expertise and his ahavat Yisrael, his love of Israel? His warmth and charm, coupled with deep understanding of the holy Torah of HaShem, were a potent combination for which we simply had no defenses; he utterly disarmed us. So we joined the ever-increasing line of Schwartzie's brand of ba'alei teshuvah, and are we ever glad we did!

THE FUTURE OF AMERICAN JEWRY

Will Your Grandchildren Be Jewish? Revisited II

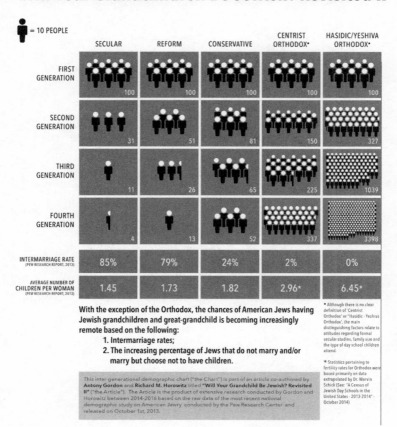

With the exception of the Orthodox, the chances of American Jews having Jewish grandchildren and great-grandchild is becoming increasingly remote based on the following:

1. Intermarriage rates;
2. The increasing percentage of Jews that do not marry and/or marry but choose not to have children.

* Although there is no clear definition of 'Centrist Orthodox' or 'Hasidic - Yeshiva Orthodox', the main distinguishing factors relate to attitudes regarding formal secular studies, family size and the type of day school children attend.

* Statistics pertaining to fertility rates for Orthodox were based primarily on data extrapolated by Dr. Marvin Schick (See: "A Census of Jewish Day Schools in the United States - 2013-2014" - October 2014)

This inter-generational demographic chart ("the Chart") is part of an article co-authored by **Antony Gordon** and **Richard M. Horowitz** titled **"Will Your Grandchild Be Jewish? Revisited II"** ("the Article"). The Article is the product of extensive research conducted by Gordon and Horowitz between 2014-2016 based on the raw data of the most recent national demographic study on American Jewry conducted by the Pew Research Center and released on October 1st, 2013.

CHAPTER 15

A VORT IZ NISHT KEIN FARFALEN

Like teachers, rabbis on university campuses typically don't get to discover what happens to the young students they encounter only for a short time. Even so, the Chabad rabbis at UCLA would strive to make every interaction positive and meaningful.

We lived with a mantra, a Yiddish saying from the Frierdiker Rebbe: "*A vort iz nisht kein farfalen*—every kind word spoken to someone was not for naught." Whether we saw the fruits of our labor or not, we trusted that our efforts would ultimately be successful, even if we didn't see success. We trusted that just saying something Jewish or positive would somehow have a positive effect. We did whatever we could to try to connect to students and Jews all over town.

There was a guy named Steve, a self-proclaimed "Jewish radical," who had a table right next to mine on Bruin Walk. We nicknamed him and his group JERKS. I would ask him to put on tefillin and Steve would reject, argue, fight, and cause me tremendous anguish and heartache. Needless to say, he never put on tefillin, and I was happy when Steve finally left UCLA.

But that wasn't the end of the story. Fast-forward to 2016, when I was sick with multiple myeloma and was being wheeled down the block by my caretaker, Allen, when I heard someone call out, "Schwartzie!" I looked up, and who was it? Steve!

Steve came over and said, "You won't believe it. I became a cantor, and I specialize in bar mitzvah lessons for autistic children. Your neighbor who has special needs is about to become bar mitzvah, and I'm his bar mitzvah teacher." He went on to say that forty years prior, he remembered my always asking him to put on the tefillin at UCLA. Then Steve asked whether he could come to my house to have me teach him—and thus his future bar mitzvah students—how to put on tefillin.

Truly, *a vort iz nisht kein farfalen*: every kind word spoken to someone was not for naught.

I also learned that a single, brief encounter could ripple endlessly, as it did for one assimilated UCLA student:

> Recently, an old friend surfaced. He had been studying for a number of years in an Israeli yeshiva for adults who had no background in Judaism.
>
> He had been a rock guitarist with a group that actually became famous after our hero left it to go to Israel.
>
> When he came back from Israel, after being ordained, he took Los Angeles by storm and developed a very large following that came to his concerts and Torah classes. One night, when we were alone, he smiled cherubically and said that he wanted to reveal a secret to me.
>
> He had been a student at UCLA; at that time his last name was Foster. (When he went to Israel, he changed it back to Finkelstein.) He once stopped at my campus info table to talk, and I asked him whether he had ever put on tefillin. He said he never even had a bar mitzvah. I whipped out my tefillin, and almost before he knew what was happening, I had it on him.
>
> He transferred schools shortly afterward and never saw me again while a student. But that on-campus quickie tefillin demonstration was his turning point. Our encounter lasted about twenty minutes.
>
> If you put out the energy, you never know!

"The students loved him. They absolutely loved him," Olivia said. "He had that ability to reach a tremendous number of people. Almost every day, no matter where we are, we run into people who say, 'I met Schwartzie for such a short time, and he changed my life.' It happens almost constantly; it's freaky how often it happens."

It really is fascinating because you don't find out about these things. You have an interaction, and that's it. You usually don't get to hear about it later. You don't know the effect you have on people.

Cantor Steve Puzarne putting on tefillin with Mendel Schwartz, more than 40 years after heckling Schwartzie at UCLA

CHAPTER 16

NEUROPSYCHIATRIC INSTITUTE, UCLA

Every year during Yom Kippur services, I spoke about the concept of *teshuvah*, correctly translated as "return." The Jewish soul is part of G-d and is connected on the deepest subconscious level of our being, whether we are aware of it or not. Therefore, becoming more observant isn't about adopting a foreign identity or set of practices. *Teshuvah*—return—is really just about getting in touch with the person you already are and returning to your true self.

In yeshiva, we studied this idea. When I was a campus rabbi at UCLA, this became a reality.

It was my first job! I was all of twenty-four and completely clueless as a campus rabbi. And why not? I was actually Chabad's first campus rabbi on planet Earth.

While serving as a rabbi on campus at UCLA, one of my regular duties was to act as a chaplain in the university hospital, which included visiting Jewish patients at NPI, the UCLA Neuropsychiatric Institute.

One day, a young man, let's call him Jeffrey, went off his medication and had a psychotic break. He became as strong as five grown men and went on a rampage, destroying the large commercial kitchen in the Chabad House. After a while, five guys tackled him and brought him across the street to UCLA Medical Center, where he was locked up in NPI.

Later, I went to visit him in the hospital. I was carrying tefillin, thinking that Jeffrey, a religious Jew, would want to put them on. Jeffrey was an older graduate student, a little older, in fact, than I was: quiet, nerdish, a bit strange, even when *on* his medication.

The lockdown area of NPI was stark and cold. Locked doors. This was where the hospital sent the "developmental disability and neurology mental patients."

People were on suicide watch and could be dangerous. Showing up with tefillin was no easy feat. People could strangle themselves. But I assured the staff that Jeffrey was a Chabad House regular and would use the tefillin as they were meant to be used.

He was estranged from his parents, and I was his only visitor. After going through a lot of security and finally being admitted, I found his room. He was lying in a small bed in a small, single room. A slim, wiry, very together-looking male nurse was feeding him a hamburger, slowly, with a metal fork.

When I walked into the tiny room, the two of them were distracted, and in that moment, Jeffrey made a quick, unexpected move. He grabbed the fork away from the nurse and held it right next to his throat! I thought I was going to see a serious amount of blood in the ensuing violence.

The nurse slowly and very calmly put his hand out and began talking to Jeffrey as if he were a third-grader. "Give me the fork, please, Jeffrey," he said, sweetly but firmly.

No one moved. I became extremely nervous, still imagining that very soon there would be a *lot* of blood.

The nurse asked for the fork a second time. Jeffrey had this very weird smile on his face.

Finally, after the third time, he said, "Please, give me the fork, Jeffrey," in a pedantic, obnoxious, authoritative tone of voice, and Jeffrey, very slowly—slow-motion slowly—handed the nurse the metal fork.

After that crisis, the chief psychiatric resident happened to be walking down the hall and passed by the open door of Jeffrey's room, where the three of us sat crowded together. By this time, I was starting to put tefillin on Jeffrey, and as the doctor passed by, Jeffrey screamed out to me, "Rabbi, *he's* Jewish—put tefillin on him!"

The resident doctor was young, possibly under thirty. When Jeffrey screamed out, "Put tefillin on him!" the doctor got a look of horror on his face and actually started to run away!

That seemed a bit strange. He was very good-looking, seemingly quite intelligent and professional. I imagined that he spent a lot of time with psychotics, so I didn't quite understand why he had run away from a perfectly sane rabbi, even one with a long red beard.

I finished my chaplaincy visit and headed for the doctor's office to learn about Jeffrey's condition. The resident ushered me in, but it was clear that he wasn't happy to see me.

I officially introduced myself and asked to hear about Jeffrey's illness. He opened a drawer and took out Jeffrey's file, started reading aloud about bipolar this and paranoid schizophrenic that. But after he had read a few lines, he put down the file, looked up at me, and said something that told me he was in big trouble: "Those are just words, rabbi; we really know very little about mental health!"

I thought to myself, "This bright Jewish fellow is really in deep trouble. He's spent the past several years of his life as a resident shrink in the very prestigious NPI, part of the very prestigious UCLA Medical Center, and now he's come to realize that his entire career isn't what he thought it was going to be."

As I was about to leave, he had a strange expression on his face and he said, "I am privy to some interesting trivia that I have never told anyone because I didn't meet anyone I thought would be as fascinated by it as I am. But I know you would."

I was intrigued. "Sure," I said.

The doctor told me that an average of five people a day flip out and are brought to NPI; few of them are Jewish. But, he said, "I have noticed that every single year around the Jewish holidays, the Jewish admittance goes up dramatically. And on one day each year, admittance spikes closer to twenty people, with fifteen of them Jewish."

"What day is that?" I asked.

The doctor said, "Yom Kippur."

And here's the punch line: each year, when admittance to NPI went up on Yom Kippur, it was on the Hebrew calendar date, the tenth day of Tishrei, not a consistent date on the secular calendar. *The Jews who were brought in on Yom Kippur didn't even know it was Yom Kippur.*

The doctor gazed at me intently. "So, I am asking you, rabbi, why is this so? How can this be?"

At that moment, I didn't know what to tell him. I did think that I should really get involved in this young Jewish man's life. But I was on the job, the first job I'd ever had, less than six months; the fellow was older than I was, and I didn't think he liked me. So, after a while, I left.

One week later, I was driving on the freeway, listening to the news on the radio, and I heard that the chief psychiatric resident at NPI, the same man who had told me about the spike in Jewish psychiatric admissions on Yom Kippur, had driven off Mulholland Drive in an apparent suicide.

That was one of my first major failures. He died before I could work with him, perhaps to get him to return to himself.

I know how to answer that young doctor's question now. What he called "trivia" in 1970 actually exposed a deep connection between Jews and the Day of Atonement. Yom Kippur is not just a theological concept, but an actual reality. It's something that a Jewish soul (even the soul of a Jew with zero Jewish background) *feels*. That's why I call Yom Kippur "the annual coming-out party for closet Jewry."

There is only one day on the Jewish calendar that the Talmud refers to as "the day:" Yom Kippur. Tractate *Yoma* in the Talmud describes how powerful "the day" is by presenting it as the day on which we Jews are all connected and open to change. We are also open to connect to our deep subconscious Jewish identity, whether we like it or not, or even whether we are aware of it or not. It's a subconscious stirring of the soul that comes to the surface, often in unexplainable ways.

Judaism tells us, *Yom Kippur m'chaper*: The day of Yom Kippur itself provides atonement to every Jewish soul. That means that while on every other of the 364 days of the year we actually need to do something to obtain atonement, the day of Yom Kippur is so holy and so powerful that the day itself provides atonement.

I call that the ultimate reality of Yom Kippur!

CHAPTER 17

PUSHING THE ENVELOPE: WANNA SHAKE MY *LULAV*?

My joyous approach to *Yiddishkeit,* which I displayed from my first days on campus, also pushed the envelope at times. I managed to raise a few eyebrows as early as 1971 with this come-on for Purim festivities:

My first year in California, I had been a campus rabbi at Cal State Northridge, then called Valley State College (which had an even more assimilated population than that of UCLA), and found that all the students had heard of Chanukah, which they thought of as Jewish Christmas, but 95 percent had *not* heard of Purim! I worked hard before Purim and managed to seduce ten students into coming to the Purim party.

The next year, before Purim, I got permission to get the mic at the free speech area where students could say literally *anything* they wanted. And they did, without the four-letter expletives.

Back in the ghettos of Brooklyn, the young Chasidim and yeshiva students would have monthly fabrengen*s*, which were kind of like group therapy sessions with some food and *l'chayim* juice (a.k.a. vodka) flowing freely, to melt down inhibitions in order to grow spiritually.

When a young Chasid overdid it with the *l'chayim* and got juiced to the gills (i.e., wasted, plastered, loaded), the innocent slang had it as, "Did you see how stoned Moshe Yankel got last night at the fabrengen?"

I really wanted a huge crowd to show up the second year for Purim, not just ten people, as in my first year. So, when I got the mic, I tried to

outrageous and charismatic as I could to get students to come. I
ceeded, but it almost cost me my job.

Two days after my speech at CSUN, I was called on the carpet by
my superior, who was holding a copy of the campus newspaper at CSUN,
called the *Sundial*, and asked in a menacingly angry tone if I had seen the
lead story on the front page. When I said I hadn't seen it yet, he handed it
to me and waited impatiently for me to finish reading it.

Unbeknownst to me, among the informal audience sitting on the
lawn listening to my impassioned, enthusiastic speech of two days prior,
had been a student journalist for the *Sundial*.

This is the quote on the front page that almost ended my career shortly
after it had begun:

*The campus rabbi demanded that everyone be strict with observing the
religious rituals of the Jewish holiday of Purim, quoting Bob Dylan to make
his point:*

EVERYBODY MUST GET STONED!

For the better part of my nineteen years as a Chabad campus rabbi, I
stationed myself in the center of the UCLA campus and offered traditional
Judaism in full living color, adding an extra element of showmanship to the
usual Chabad spiel.

It was also where, away from the cozy Lubavitcher nest at 770 Eastern
Parkway in Brooklyn, I first met large numbers of young Jews who had
grown up unmoored from their parents' Jewish roots in New York, Boston,
Chicago and other points east. Their families were as likely to have let go
of tradition—going to synagogue, making Shabbat, keeping *mitzvot* big
and small—as they were to have held on to it, and the concept of the
"Jewish neighborhood" had pretty much fallen by the wayside as well—not
to mention the notorious distractions of 1960s popular entertainment and
counterculture, of which I was well aware.

More than 90 percent of the students who approached me came over
to me with an apologetic disclaimer. It went something like this:

—Rabbi, I'm not a good Jew, but I have a question . . .

—Rabbi, I'm a bad Jew, but I need to ask you a question . . .

—Rabbi, I would never talk to someone like you, but I have a question
. . .

That last one was always my favorite.

The questions with which these college students had annoyed their parents and childhood rabbis were my bread and butter. And if I got the students closer to their parents' faith, that was the full meal!

When I first came to Los Angeles to be a campus rabbi, I worked at UCLA for the first year. The second year, I decided to do something more challenging. UCLA had nine thousand Jewish students (out of thirty-three thousand) and more than twenty on-campus Jewish student organizations; a Jewish student newspaper called *Ha'am*, "The People," came along later. But California State University at Northridge (CSUN), fifteen miles north, in the San Fernando Valley, only had four thousand Jewish students (out of twenty-eight thousand) and was a commuter school with only one small dorm, so it was more difficult to connect with my unsuspecting Jewish clientele.

After a year of relatively great success at JewCLA (our code name), I started going to CSUN two days a week, starting at the beginning of the school year, when all the High Holidays occur. It was difficult, but I received permission to set up a sukkah on campus. The sukkah turned out to be something of an attraction, if only because the Valley can be *hot* in early October. Plus, I put large amounts of honey cake and drinks on the table in the sukkah, so students would enter, and I'd invite them for some great munchies and cold beverages.

After a while, I'd whip out a *lulav* and *etrog* (the combined palm, willow, and myrtle fronds and the citron—Sukkot ritual objects) and ask whether they'd like to observe the biblical commandment to perform the ritual for the holiday. Most didn't know it was a Jewish holiday. Many had never seen a sukkah, let alone actually been in one or eaten in one, and many had never seen a lulav and etrog, and certainly had never fulfilled the *mitzvah* of shaking the lulav.

The sukkah was in the free speech area, where there were a number of information tables staffed by students. One table was a Jewish table with information about Israel and Jewish social events. About seven Jewish kids sat behind the table, just hanging out.

I knew that even though these students were some of the most committed Jews on campus, publicly identifying as Jews, they had not done the ritual of the "four species," one of the commandments mandated in the Bible for the holiday of Sukkot. I also knew that if the first student I asked to do it refused, I wouldn't get a crowd to line up to do it, as students typically follow the leader. These kids were sitting at a Jewish table, but to actually perform a biblical precept was considered "religious," therefore uncool, and at that time, the worst contemporary social sin was to be considered uncool. It was inscribed in the student Decalogue: "THOU SHALT NOT BE UNCOOL!"

As I approached the Jewish students' table with my long beard, holding the tall palm branch and the large, lemon-like fruit, I caught the leader's eye, and he began to react with an expression just a little less extreme than horror. He definitely was not going to be the first. What was I going to say?

Finally, in desperation and frustration, I stood beside the table and hollered:

"Anybody wanna shake my lulav?"

Everyone stopped talking. There was a pregnant pause. Suddenly, a cute, short-haired blonde coed piped up loudly, "I'll do it! I don't know what it is, but I'll do it!" After a short explanation that was loud enough for all of them to hear (and by this time they were all listening attentively), the leader from the Jewish table came over to do it; then all the rest lined up. I felt the Rebbe's blessing pumping strongly despite my insecurity and trepidation as I led the group into the sukkah.

That little blonde student was extremely clueless about her religion; neither she nor her young parents (both Jewish) knew *anything* about Judaism. But we became instant best buddies and remained quite close for her four years as an undergrad. She got deeply involved with Judaism, and much to her very assimilated parents' surprise and dismay, she became quite traditional. I eventually officiated at her wedding to a funky, shy, geeky Jewish guy, and she had two children before they moved to Virginia for his work.

Another time, I was near the sukkah at CSUN and saw a huge guy, about six foot one, two-hundred fifty pounds, walking in. What was somewhat shocking was that he was wearing a kipah. At UCLA, there were always about thirty to forty kipah-wearing guys, but at CSUN, there were maybe two or three. I trotted into the sukkah quickly, lest I miss him.

He told me that he had just came back from his first visit to Israel and, although he knew virtually zip about Judaism, he felt so great about Israel that he decided to wear a kipah full time. He didn't know about the mitzvah to shake the lulav. I started giving him the abridged version of the explanation of the ancient ritual, and he said, "No, there's only us here, and I have time now—explain to me the whole thing before I do it." Needless to say, I did, and we became very good friends for the next four years.

Then there was the time I went to Berkeley for Sukkot and was shaking the *lulav* with a guy who was mostly naked (that's why they call it Berzerkley). The following week, I went to New York for Simchat Torah and joined the crowd at the Rebbe's Torah processions in front of Lubavitcher headquarters in Brooklyn. And who was in that crowd? The mostly naked guy, this time with clothes on. He never left 770 Eastern Parkway after that; he became a full-on ba'al teshuvah living in Crown Heights.

Yaakov Levy had a life-changing encounter with Schwartzie at UCLA:

I was a seventeen-year-old freshman, and I did not like UCLA— too big, too impersonal. I was walking down the hill and at the bottom saw this trailer with a sukkah on it. I had not had much experience in sukkahs, even with a good Orthodox after-school education. I asked Schwartzie, "What's that?" He replied enthusiastically, "A Sukkahmobile!" Then, of course, he asked me if I wanted to make the brachah. "Sure," I said.

We climbed up the steps into the Sukkahmobile and I told him I didn't know what to do. He gave me the four species and said something. I don't recall what he said exactly, but I remember the feeling. He was smiling and said something about the meaning of the four species and the prayer, and . . . it was a transcendent moment. I cry just remembering it. Looking at his smiling, gentle face, holding the four species in the Sukkahmobile—it was this incredible moment. Time stopped. The awful anomie of UCLA vanished, and there was this connection. Schwartzie sparked a vertical and horizontal connection in my Jewish soul. It was almost forty years ago and I still remember it.

Many years later, when I learned that the sukkah represents the ananei hakavod, the clouds of glory that appeared to the Israelites in the wilderness, that indescribable special feeling in the sukkah made perfect sense to me. Maybe that's what Schwartzie tapped into. That image of him smiling right at me and holding the four species, telling me what it meant that I was about to do . . . Here I am, forty years later, deeply moved telling about it.

CHAPTER 18

WOMEN'S LIBERATION MOVEMENT, AND THE WOMEN'S MINYAN

In the early days, a Hillel rabbi named Moshe Adler served at Cal State Northridge. His wife at that time was Rachel Adler—a genius, brilliant. She grew up Reform, but she graduated from Yeshiva University and married an Orthodox rabbi. At the same time, Rachel was living as an Orthodox *rebbetzin*, going to the mikvah, the whole thing, but she was also deeply into the women's liberation movement.

In those days, at any campus you went to, one of the biggest issues was women's rights—and traditional Judaism took a big hit because it was seen as sexist. We Chabadniks were getting clobbered wherever we turned. We had no place to go. We went to do outreach and got killed, attacked viciously from all sides. The counselors, the teachers would tell the students what to ask. Ask the rabbi about *shelo asani ishah,* the blessing in which men praise G-d for not making them women. (The professors, it seemed, had never heard of any other blessings.) What about how women can't have an aliyah, can't be counted in the minyan, and can't be rabbis? Everybody knew those catchphrases, and we were getting killed.

But there was this Orthodox woman, Rachel Adler, who was a leader in the Jewish student community at Northridge. There were thousands of there; after UCLA, it had the largest number of Jews on any campus in Los Angeles.

I was teaching the *Tanya* at Rachel's house. She and her husband participated, and I was becoming closer to them. I determined that she was a powerful leader. She took women to the mikvah with her when she went, so I thought that if I were to get her on my side, I'd be able to get the rest of the people.

So, I said to Rachel Adler, "We're going to make a women's *shabbaton*. We're going to make a women's minyan, and you're going to lead the service." Because she knew everything. She was a genius. I figured, she'll come, she'll do the whole shtick on the other side of the *mechitzah,* and we'll find out how we can do it according to *halachah* (Jewish law), because she was really committed to wearing a *tallis* (prayer shawl), which was considered male clothing and not for women. We'll do it like that, all women, and it'll be the woman's *shabbaton*.

It almost happened like that.

But after it was already planned, Rabbi Cunin said, *Shailes haRav*: "Ask the Rav." Hence we explained the whole thing to Rabbi Zalman Shimon Dvorkin, Chabad's chief adviser on halachah in Crown Heights. And his answer was that it was OK. Done. It's kosher. You can have a women's minyan. There are a few conditions, this and that.

Friday morning, the women's minyan was about to take place. Thirty-five women said they were coming. Rachel's ready with the tallis. Suddenly, Rabbi Cunin said, "We never told the Rebbe what Rabbi Dvorkin said, so let's tell him."

OK. I called and told the Rebbe what we had planned (and promoted with great fanfare) and that the Rav, Rabbi Dvorkin, had said it's OK; it's kosher; it's *al pi halachah,* in accordance with Jewish law. The answer came back a few hours before Shabbat: The Rebbe said, "The Reform movement also started *al pi halachah."* That meant he had a problem with the women's *shabbaton*; he was comparing it to something the Reform movement would do. Rabbi Cunin said, "I don't know what we're going to do, but we're not going to have any women's Shabbat here. It's not happening."

To this day, I'm not sure what the Rebbe's reservation was. He wasn't antagonistic toward the Reform movement; he referred to Reform rabbis as rabbis and showed them tremendous respect. He was known to believe that women's minyans were kosher; in fact, I knew that from Rabbi Dvorkin. I think that perhaps the Rebbe was just being very, very careful because, although something may be allowed according to halachah, it may lead to something that *isn't* allowed according to halachah. Or he may have supported women's minyans in theory but had not wanted Chabad *shluchim* (emissaries) specifically to sponsor them.

Now I had to tell Rachel Adler that we weren't going to have the women's minyan. Even at that time, she had written many articles for Jewish magazines, articles of commentary, and two essays that were very positive about the mikvah. She was an extremely articulate and well-regarded person. I thought we were going to get killed and that she was going to smear Lubavitch. It was going to be terrible.

But instead, a miracle happened. All Rachel said was, "Can I still wear my tallit?" No repercussions. The women came to the regular service. They were on the other side of the *mechitzah*. Rachel wore her tallis, but she did it quietly. She went on to give *divrei* Torah, good ones. It wasn't the way it was originally planned, but it showed that we took women seriously. Rachel could have trashed us, but she didn't. A miracle.

Kicking off the
Sukkot campaign at
UCLA, 1971

Tefillin campaign, 1971

Getting "stoned" on Purim

Happy Purim

DANCE! ✦

Flyer advertising our first
Simchat Torah dance party

Live, laugh, "Lechayim" at
the rowdiest, ritual, revelry
this side of Brooklyn. Dance
and feel the vibes of over
500 M.O.T.'s* or just lay
back and get off on the
contact high ("Chasidic"
dancing is the way to revive,
revitalize and recycle the
mind and bod and is learned
by *instant* osmosis). We will
utilize high decibel voice,
"Vino" truth serum and
kosher honeycake to get the
juices flowing.

*Members of the Tribe

Tuesday, October 20, from 7 til 10 pm.
(For Conservative, Reform & Non-Affiliates!)
Chabad House, 641 Gayley, Westwood

FREE

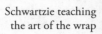

Schwartzie teaching the art of the wrap

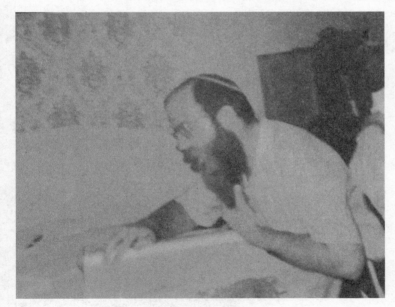

Taking a few minutes for private study

JEWISH WOMEN

Flyer for event discussing Jewish women

Is Judaism sexist? Is feminism kosher?
What is Jewish mysticism?
What about reincarnation?
G–d, soul-mates, etc., etc. Hear and talk to

MANIS FRIEDMAN
Director of the
Women's Institute of Jewish Studies

THURSDAY, Feb. 15 at 8:00 P.M.

CHABAD HOUSE
741 Gayley Ave., Westwood

FREE
(men welcome)

Schwartzie teaching at UCLA

CHAPTER 19

CROSS-COUNTRY ROAD TRIP '73

In 1972, Soviets started trickling out from behind the Iron Curtain. There was a mega-philanthropist named Finkelstein who had been approached by the Los Angeles Jewish Federation, which informed him that there were three hundred Soviet families leaving the country and that Los Angeles was going to absorb them. Finkelstein, who had a relationship with Chabad, told the Federation that he needed to speak to Rabbi Cunin.

Cunin told Finkelstein that with four million dollars, he could take care of the families and the future emigration of Soviet families leaving the Soviet Union. Finkelstein agreed.

My partner and good friend Rabbi Yerachmiel Stillman told Cunin that he had a vibrant and charismatic Russian Chabad friend who had just emigrated from the Soviet Union and was currently living in Crown Heights. This is how Rabbi Naftoli Estulin and his wife, Fayge, came to Los Angeles.

Naftoli had mentioned to the Rebbe that he wanted to work for Rabbi Gershon Mendel Gorelik, who had recently opened a kosher restaurant in Italy to attract Jewish travelers and to service the Chasidic Polish Jews doing business there.

The Rebbe responded, "Don't bother me with this; G-d didn't make a miracle for you to leave Russia so you can spend your life being a *mashgiach* (kosher supervisor) in a restaurant." Shortly thereafter, Naftoli received our request to work in California for the soon-to-be Russian community, to which the Rebbe agreed.

The bad news was, after Naftoli and his wife arrived in Los Angeles, Finkelstein went bankrupt, and, moreover, Soviets weren't getting out. So, Naftoli joined me, Rabbi Avramel Levitansky (Chabad Rabbi of Santa Monica), Stillman, and Cunin in Westwood. One day a week, Naftoli assisted Levitansky with his after-school program for children. Another day of the week, he hung out with Cunin, and another day of the week I would bring Naftoli to UCLA. We all loved Naftoli. I would showcase him on Bruin Walk for the college students to meet a real live Russian rabbi who was a recent refusenik. He didn't speak a word of English. He was the real deal.

Naftoli eventually moved from Westwood and initiated a new synagogue on Fairfax Avenue, near Canter's delicatessen, for the Orthodox community there. It was bashert that he did, as the following year, Soviet Jews started arriving in Los Angeles and moved in large numbers to West Hollywood. Naftoli was their man. He had a small school bus and picked up Soviet families from LAX every week. He became the spiritual leader for thousands of Soviet kids. He had day camps, adult activities, soup kitchens, and so on. He also was responsible for thousands of Soviet children being circumcised. Nobody was circumcised in the Soviet Union. I myself served as the *sandek* (unofficial godfather) for some of these kids. Many years later, my children worked as counselors at his day camp. My daughter, Rick, was married in his newly built, state-of-the-art synagogue in the center of West Hollywood.

Rabbi Naftoli reminisced: Before I left Westwood to open my center on Fairfax Avenue, my son, Chaim, was born. I wasn't doing much, as the Russians still hadn't arrived. So, I decided to advertise and make a big to-do for the first bris of a Russian refusenik in Los Angeles. I wanted the entire city to know that in Russia it was prohibited to perform this ritual, but here in Los Angeles we were allowed. And this would encourage others to be more open to Judaism. My boss nixed the idea. He said it'll be a balagan, a lot of chaos, and this extra noise is not necessary. So, I wrote to the Rebbe in New York and complained. The Rebbe told me, "You should listen to your superior, but don't worry, as you'll be making a lot of noise with thousands of circumcisions soon." He knew before I did that the Russians were coming.

In the summer of 1973, I encountered the Gross family. The family arrived from Ukraine with five kids and was nervous about the Jewish landscape in Los Angeles. Many families from the former Soviet Union were not that interested in Jewish survival for their families and children, but the Grosses were extremely nervous about this. They approached us, but we had no day camps at that time for their teenage kids. We decided they should all go to the East Coast, as there were many overnight camps for Jewish children in upstate New York, the Borscht Belt. There were other kids as well who wanted a Jewish summer experience. We had a total of twelve teenagers on our hands with no game plan. It was decided, to save money, that Naftoli and I would drive his small bus from California to New York with these twelve kids. The parents agreed—nobody signed waivers in those days—and we prepared and packed food for our group for the one-week drive across the country.

As it turned out, our jalopy minibus was fit to drive to and from LAX airport. It was not built for travel to New York. Sure enough, it gave out in Albuquerque, New Mexico. There we were, with all this food in the back, twelve kids, and Naftoli and I stuck in the middle of nowhere. Half the kids wanted to get the bus fixed or find another one and keep going to New York, while the others wanted to return home to Los Angeles.

So, we called the Rebbe from a pay phone in Albuquerque and asked what we should do. The Rebbe responded that the girls who wanted to return to Los Angeles should take a flight back, and the girls who wanted to have the summer experience in New York should take a flight to New York.

We finally made it to New York and prepared the kids for the overnight camp.

I'm glad we did, too, because it brought about a *shidduch*. Twenty-one-year-old Esther Gross, one of the girls who wanted to continue the journey to the East Coast, met Zalman Roth, a new ba'al teshuvah in Crown Heights, on that trip. I'd met Zalman in Los Angeles, and I asked him if he'd like to meet a "commie chick" from Ukraine. Zalman said he was open to giving it a try, and that's how he met Esther Gross, now Esther Roth. They went on to have lots of children and grandchildren.

I love when that happens!

CHAPTER 20

YENTL, WHERE ARE YOU?

My First Encounter with a Cross-Dressing Girl

One day, Chabad House in Westwood got a call for help from a fifteen-year-old wannabe ba'al teshuvah, a secular Jew seeking to become religious. Let's call him Aaron.

He told us that his father wasn't Jewish, but his mom was, and, as such, he knows to which ethnicity and faith he is obligated. Now, his mom was divorced from his biological dad, but she was living with an alcoholic Native American who liked to beat her.

Aaron started becoming interested in traditional Judaism because there was an incredibly nice, almost-Orthodox rabbi in his hometown, Cupertino, California, and our hero had started becoming observant in Cupertino. But the mother's live-in boyfriend, who absolutely did not like Jews, beat up Aaron and broke his ribs. The rabbi and Aaron decided that Aaron should move away from this physical danger.

Therefore, that nice, almost-Orthodox rabbi (from a very Orthodox upbringing and background) called upon us to adopt the troubled teen boy who wanted a black hat for his sixteenth birthday, and he came down to Los Angeles and took up residence in the Chabad House building.

There were a few strange things that we really didn't pay attention to.

If someone is growing in the practice of Chasidism, after a while, he goes to the mikvah (ritual bath) before praying or putting on the tallis and tefillin. Aaron consistently refused to immerse in the mikvah with his fellow Chasidim, saying that his broken ribs hadn't healed and that a doctor told him that he couldn't have a bath while his ribs were still broken.

Also, there was Aaron's behavior at the farbrengens. Usually a Chasidic fabrengen involved a little Torah study, a lot of singing, and a certain amount of drinking. Vodka flowed freely, and no one got carded. When Aaron started participating strongly in the *l'chaim*s, the toasts, and then got very emotional, we all figured he certainly had things to cry about. But that was also a little strange.

However, Aaron was extremely bright and had already gone through many of life's worst challenges. He was a great Torah student, soaking it up like a sponge. We started dreaming about getting him a scholarship to one of the "Ivy League" yeshivas on the East Coast.

Aaron would be the darling of the dorm: the baby-faced kid who was really smart and came from zero family background. Plus, he really seemed to be way more mature than any other fifteen-year-old was.

I had relatives in Long Beach, so, one Shabbat, we went there. On Saturday night, I got a frantic phone call from the associate rabbi with a shocking announcement:

Aaron was a *she,* not a *he.*

There had been a fabrengen on Shabbat, as usual, and, as usual, Aaron got drunk, but this time he threw up on himself and actually passed out.

The associate Rabbi always helped those who got too happy on alcohol, so he dragged Aaron into the bathroom to undress him and clean him up.

Guess what part of Aaron's body he couldn't find?

It wasn't there. She was missing an essential part for any male yeshiva student.

In retrospect, many formerly strange things began to make sense.

Now we decided to call her Aharona, but she retained the costume of a yeshiva student: white shirt, black suit, black shoes, and black fedora.

At that time, there was a very successful psychiatrist who worked in Beverly Hills named Sy Applebaum. The almost-Orthodox rabbi from Cupertino came down to Los Angeles, and we decided to call Dr. Applebaum to intervene in a case of gender blurring, but we never had the chance to meet with him.

Another two days passed, and Aharona was gone. I am happy that she was discovered before she became a resident of the men's dorm in a yeshiva in Montreal or the like.

But I never found out what happened to her.

Yentl, where are you?

CHAPTER 21

THE *BA'AL TESHUVA* REVOLUTION

"America Is No Different"

This was the surprising verdict in 1941 of the previous Lubavitcher Rebbe, Joseph Isaac Schneerson, then the leader of the Chabad Lubavitch movement. I say this was a surprising verdict because the general thinking about the United States, the *Goldene Medinah*, the land whose streets are paved with gold, was that this country was somehow different. Orthodoxy, many maintained, would never flourish in the United States because this society was unlike anything observant Jews had ever known.

Not so, the previous Rebbe said. The same way we practiced our religion in Warsaw, in Moscow, in the underground movement, and in Europe is exactly how we will practice it here. America is no different. Because of that attitude, Chabad was instrumental from the start in infusing Judaism amongst the Jewish people living in the New York area and up and down the East Coast. Just because this is a land of freedom doesn't mean that we take off our *kipot*, we don't keep kosher, and so on. Chabad therefore learned its mission of opening synagogues, schools, and other necessities in communities spreading outward from New York.

When Rabbi Menachem Mendel Schneerson became the Rebbe in 1951, he took the teaching of the previous Rebbe (his father in-law) and multiplied it to the nth degree. He spoke about the necessity of teaching Jews who don't know the difference between an *alef* and a *bet* in the Hebrew alphabet. He said that even though not all of us are rabbis, we all have the potential to teach another Jew about the difference between those two letters. That's where the real sharing of what you could call the "Jewish gospel" began. It started in Brooklyn and the Lower East Side and eventually spread across the United States and the world.

At the time, even those people who still wore their kipot in the home might take them off when they ventured outside. They would be Jews in their living rooms and "Americans" in the street. The Rebbe cautioned that this was not the right way to go, that we could and should be fully observant and proud Jews in all places and at all times. For Jews who had searing memories of rejection, violence, and abuse at the hands of gentiles in Eastern Europe, the idea of going up to talk to total strangers and essentially advertising one's Judaism seemed like a dangerous concept.

Today, you can find a Chabad rabbi with his wife and family in virtually every corner of the globe, offering minyanim, classes, kosher food, schools, mikvahs, and every other accoutrement of Jewish life. But initially, many Orthodox communities were resistant to the idea of sending their children essentially into the unknown, where they would live far from the comfort and strength of their own homes back in Brooklyn. Little by little, however, the numbers changed, and now Jewish "outreach" is everywhere.

This teaching of the previous Rebbe in 1941 and the Rebbe in 1951 is what we call the Ba'al Teshuvah Revolution: finding Jews who are "distant" from Judaism and bringing them back into the fold.

A great example of living Jewish life publicly was Chabad's *Lag Ba'omer* parades, held on public streets, which the Rebbe intended as a proclamation of the fact that Jews have the right to be proud to be Jewish. All this took place against the backdrop of a rapidly increasing assimilation rate, so it's easy to see that Chabad, and the other individuals and institutions it had inspired, have all been instrumental in maintaining the growth and actually building toward the future for the Jewish people.

When we think about the idea of the Rebbe's mission of growing Jewish identity, pride, knowledge, and behavior, we usually think about the people who were approached by young men in the ubiquitous "mitzvah tanks"—asking if they had put on tefillin that day or, if they were women, if they were going to light Shabbat candles that Friday night, and so on.

Initially, however, the real resistance came from the Orthodox Jews in Crown Heights and the Lower East Side. They didn't think it was such a great idea to approach college kids who were not dressed appropriately or to go into the streets to try to "nab" a Jew and talk to him or her about religious practice. This did not sit well with many individuals, and despite the Rebbe's guidance, many people were initially against it. The Rebbe actually had to handle disputes with other rabbis in other Orthodox communities, not just individuals within the Chabad fold.

Today, it seems hard to believe that Modern Orthodox or ultra-Orthodox Jews would look upon the notion of kiruv, or bringing Jews close to Judaism, as something odd or even unacceptable. But back in the 1950s, when the Rebbe first began to promulgate these ideas, resistance was fierce. The sense was that Jews should just stay in their own community and be the best they could be. Who could imagine the Satmar Rebbe from Williamsburg putting tefillin on a secular Jew? It took time for the idea to take hold.

Jewish identity spiked after the Six-Day War in 1967. Now other organizations and charismatic leaders had joined the kiruv movement. You had individuals like Rebbetzin Esther Jungreis with the establishment of Hineini in 1973, Rabbi Noach Weinberg with the founding of Aish HaTorah in 1974, and, of course, Rabbi Shlomo Carlebach, to name just a few.

THE PASSING OF SCHWARTZIE'S WIFE ALTA SHULA AND HIS MARRIAGE TO OLIVIA SCHWARTZ

After just a few years on the job as one of the first Chabad rabbis doing Jewish outreach, Schwartzie, father of seven small children, lost his twenty-nine-year-old wife, Alta Shula, to an undiagnosed heart ailment. She collapsed at the wedding of a dear friend in California. Initially, the doctors thought it was heart failure, but it was most likely a ruptured aneurysm. No autopsy was ever performed.

Schwartzie had just begun to make a name for himself as a leader in the kiruv movement and as an icon for many other rabbis to follow suit. This was terrible news in all communities, especially in California. Schwartzie himself was devastated.

He knew he could not leave seven kids without a mother. About six months after Alta Shula's death, Schwartzie was contacted by Rabbi Manis Friedman, dean of an all-girls school in Minnesota called Bais Chana. Rabbi Friedman knew all about ba'al teshuvah girls, which included some young women in their thirties who were becoming observant through his school. Schwartzie later recalled, "Rabbi Friedman told me, 'I have good news and bad news. The good news is that I have three girls whom you could potentially date.' He went on: 'The bad news is that they're all living in Crown Heights, and they're all roommates, which means that if it doesn't work out with the first one, she's going to talk about you to the other two, and you're done.'"

Schwartzie agreed to meet one of the women anyway.

If ever a couple was bashert, it was Shlomo Schwartz and Olivia Cantor.

Born in Cedarhurst, New York, one of the very Jewish Five Towns of Long Island, Olivia was almost a stereotype of a kind of Jewish girl who came of age in the late 1960s. Photos from the early '70s show a smiling young woman with huge hoop earrings and thick, wavy red hair streaming down her back under a kerchief. She began college with a fierce determination to stand up for peace and to be a voice of reason in an era of uncertainty.

After studying Buddhist and Hindu philosophy in school, Olivia spent most of her twenties on the road, spending time in Israel and Europe before landing at an ashram in India. She studied for three years with a woman guru who turned out to be Jewish-born and who "told me that Judaism was the highest spiritual path in the world, and if I was a spiritual seeker, I should go to Israel and find out what it means to serve G-d."

She began Torah studies on a religious moshav, which only whetted her appetite for a more immersive experience. "The more that I opened up to loving being Jewish and to understanding the depth and the commitment of a Jewish spiritual path, the more I fell in love with the land of Israel, and the more my heart opened to it."

Looking for a seminary, she found the Diaspora Yeshiva in the Old City of Jerusalem and stayed for more than four years. "It

*was really quite an interesting time in terms of Jewish spiritu-
ality," Olivia said. "Diaspora Yeshiva at the time had extremely
creative people—writers and musicians." It also taught Jews who
had experiences with Eastern philosophies and practiced yoga.
Olivia had a number of teachers from Chasidic backgrounds and
returned to the States wanting to learn more about Chasidut.*

*A meeting with the Lubavitcher Rebbe and enrollment in the
Minnesota seminary of Rabbi Manis Friedman pulled into focus
the rigorous Jewish ritual and practice Olivia had absorbed in
Jerusalem. Chasidut, she realized, was her correct spiritual path.*

"I was only at the women's seminary a year before I met Shlomo," Olivia recounts. "Rabbi Friedman is the one who called me and asked me if I would go out with Shlomo. I happened to be in New York at the time and living in New York for the year, and then I went to California to visit my brother, and that's when I met Shlomo. It was like an old-fashioned shidduch.

"My first impression was positive, since I kept going out with him. I was visiting in California, my brother in Northern California, and I had friends, very good friends, from Israel who were living in Los Angeles, and I went to stay with them. That's where I dated Shlomo from.

"In the Chasidic world, dating is really on two levels. Level one is, of course, you want to go out and have fun and like a person in any other dating situation, but on the other level, it's about looking toward the future. It's, 'Are there enough things in common? Is this a goal, a path, a person I want to be with?' I'm looking potentially for a marriage partner, so it's not just to go out and have fun. But it really becomes dating like any other type of dating situation in which you're eager to go out and you have a good time. Certainly, we didn't go out to eat, as there were really no kosher restaurants at that time in Los Angeles, but, you know, we drove around and we went to pretty places.

"Our wedding was a lot of fun. We got married in Crown Heights in front of 770 Eastern Parkway. We had maybe 150 people who came. I had already been living in New York a year, and I had friends who came from Israel because I had been living there many years. At the time, my parents were living in New York. Shlomo's mother was alive and his two sisters. Shlomo Carlebach was there, and we had a lot of music—a huge amount of music. We were both extremely into music. Shlomo's father was a chazzan, as were his grandfather and great-grandfather and great-great-grandfather; he's from a very long lineage of chazzanut. We had a lot of music at the wedding, and it was just a lot of fun.

"For my family, it was the first Chasidic wedding they'd ever been to. I have parents who are extremely open. My cousins were in shock, but my parents just loved every minute of it. They loved everything. My mother was so excited when she met all of the kids. The kids didn't come to the wedding, but my mother was just in seventh heaven. So we got married in New York, we came back to California, we went on a little honeymoon, and then we were living in Westwood.

"In terms of raising children, we always had live-in help; we always had full-time help. Shlomo's clarity, in terms of my being the children's mother, was 100 percent there. And our family is probably unique, in that it's one of the few families that has been in this type of situation where there is no separation at all between children from first and second marriages. And that really was due to Shlomo.

"Shlomo was an extremely hands-on father. The only thing he did not do was change diapers, but all my boys are expert diaper changers. He did everything else. It was never like today, I see people negotiating, OK, you stay up, and I'll nap. No, he was never like that. If I wanted to nap, he was with the kids. He drove all the carpools; I hated driving carpools. He did a tremendous amount of the shopping. He never, ever would not do something.

"He never said, 'I can't do it.' He might forget. I was running a retreat once, and I got a call from two of my kids, Berry and Cobi, who at the time were like five and eight, and they were waiting on a street corner on Sunday for like two hours to be picked up. I called Shlomo and said, 'Where are you?' Oh, he forgot, he's on his way to a wedding two hours away. He often would forget these things.

THE BA'AL TESHUVA REVOLUTION

"The kids had such long connections with him. He was so involved with his grandkids and his kids. He really took tremendous enjoyment from it; he wasn't a person who had kids, then that's it. I never felt that it was on my shoulders. I traveled a lot—for years before we started going to Israel together. I went every year and he took over all the responsibilities. He never, ever would say no. I wouldn't even think that I'd have to ask. He was always happy if I was doing something that made me happy."

"Shlomo was always cooperative. We went to Europe, to Ukraine, and to places he never thought he would go. I love to travel. I absolutely am a very big traveler. I spend every fall in India for three weeks, after the holidays. And if I would have asked him to come, he would have. The only reason I never took him to India was because the roads where I was going were so difficult; it was four hours of torture and he couldn't do it.

"Even if he wasn't interested in going somewhere, he was open if he was asked to look into it, if he was asked to try it out. He would always say yes. He spoke in Europe a few times: two or three years in Amsterdam for an organization called European Center for Jewish Students and once in Vienna. The students loved him. They absolutely loved him; he really had that ability to reach tremendous numbers of people.

"One of the things about Shlomo is that he was never not learning. Constantly, from morning till night, he learned. He never, ever watched television; we never went to movies. He basically didn't read secular books. Everything he did was learning Torah."

As Schwartzie's son Mendel tells it, "As you can imagine, Olivia's parents and many of her friends must have thought she was out of her mind for marrying a Chasidic rabbi with seven children, of whom the oldest was both blind and mentally disabled. There was also some backlash that Schwartzie was marrying too quickly and that he should wait a little bit longer. My father wasn't looking to date for the sake of dating. But he did realize that he needed a mother for his children.

"In fact, Olivia, whom I call my mother, brought many new ideas into the Jewish outreach apparatus and Chasidic communities with her progressive and liberal feminist background. She did so within the parameters of Jewish law. She was actually able to break a lot of barriers in Orthodoxy by having an all-woman division within The Chai Center. Previously, it had been taboo for Chasidic women to speak in front of both women and men, or even to have all-women events. Yet Olivia did this at The Chai Center, where she continues to have an all-women shabbaton, as well as events at the Dead Sea in Israel and Desert Hot Springs in California. When my mother entered the Chasidic community back in 1977, the default role of women was essentially to remain in the kitchen and raise a family. In addition to Olivia's raising the seven children my father brought into the marriage, and then having five more with my father, she became a real partner and renegade in the ba'al teshuvah movement. By bringing her feminist twist into the Chasidic world, she became a guru for hundreds, if not thousands, of women who look up to her. She certainly deserves acclaim for the choices she made and the many people she has served."

Our family-size vehicle

Marriage to Olivia. Olivia's father, left, looks on

With Shlomo Carlebach, guru in Jewish outreach

Sheva brachot: Post-wedding party in Westwood, 1978

Rabbi Mendel Futerfas, Rabbi Raichik, Rabbi Cunin delivering a talk at our Sheva Brachot, and Chabad House Chef Zack Miller.

Olivia and her adoring groom

THE CHAI CENTER: FOR ANY JEW THAT MOVES

CHAPTER 22

A MAN AHEAD OF HIS TIME?: FORMING THE CHAI CENTER

By the early 1980s, I was growing tired of chafing against the literal black-and-white nature of Chabad supervision, and the campus experience was also becoming a bit "been there, done that." When I started in Los Angeles, I was in my early twenties, a young, new dad, like many of the graduate students I encountered. By 1988, when I left UCLA, I was in my forties, with a flock of twelve kids and much less in common with college students.

At the same time, I continued to see young people—today's young generation is called millennials—as the core constituency of my mission as an emissary. During a time in which between 40 and 50 percent of Jews were marrying gentiles, I wanted young Jewish men and women marrying each other, and I was willing to move heaven and earth to help G-d make it happen.

"These people need connectivity," said Mayshe, who brought his father's model to The Chai Center of Boston. "In high school, you have NFTY and USY; college has Hillel and Chabad. You graduate, people are getting married later, and the divorce rate is up. You have this eighteen-, fifteen-year gap of any Jewish connectivity once people graduate from college, and there's no Jewish life for them. If you're married and you have a kid and you're really traditional, you'll think about joining some temple somewhere. But how many of those young adults, especially if you're single, actually join one?"

I realized that they weren't going to come to the synagogue; they're not becoming members. So, well ahead of the Chabad curve, I started organizing parties for Jewish singles.

These innovations ran counter to the European model of Jewish communal practice that Chabad followed.

In the old template, Jews went to synagogue daily, and your wife and kids would come on Saturday. I felt we had it wrong. No one's signing up for membership. We had to go to clubs and rent out auditoriums and make wild parties and huge Passover seders. We really had to reach out and find our Jewish brethren. This obviously didn't sit well with establishment thinking at that time. Even my close friend Rabbi Shlomo Carlebach of blessed memory, whose liturgical music has been a constant across the Jewish spectrum since the 1960s, was too edgy for the Chabad establishment.

The massive, boisterous events I arranged were a jarring element to my Chabad superiors, especially my immediate boss, Rabbi Shlomo Cunin, who had brought me to Los Angeles.

The second element of tension between my superiors and me at Chabad was my insistence on conducting High Holidays services in English: my position was that almost all the people who showed up for holiday services didn't know Hebrew and wouldn't know what the rabbi and cantor were saying. For the "once-a-year Jew" who doesn't understand a word of Hebrew to finally make it to synagogue and then be forced to sit for hours and hours painfully bored and lost in the service—in my opinion, this was a disaster. I felt these services were actually driving Jews even further away from Judaism. I wanted everyone to go through, page by page, in English and have a meaningful experience. I defended my position that G-d is a linguist. Cunin and Chabad thought I was losing my mind and becoming too progressive.

We butted heads for a long time.

I snuck money under the table from Chabad's bookkeeper for these singles parties I was hosting. I barely got a minyan on Shabbat, but these singles parties were wildly successful beyond my imagination. I was holding them on Sunday nights. When Cunin asked me about these debits from the account, I told him it was for the *melaveh malkas,* the gatherings on Saturday evenings. This went on for two years.

> *Schwartzie's son-in-law Jacob Shallman recounted: "Rabbi Cunin wanted to control Schwartzie's style and approach, and Schwartzie didn't like that. It came to a head when a Purim party he threw swelled to the largest one in the city, about a thousand students, boys and girls. Rabbi Cunin thought it was out of control and not halachically appropriate and basically told him to cancel the party. Schwartzie refused, and it was just kind of downhill from then. There was a clash of egos: Rabbi Cunin said he'd fire him, Schwartzie said he'd quit, and it just ended."*

After leaving UCLA, I continued as a Chabad rabbi, moving from the UCLA campus area to Mar Vista, a Los Angeles neighborhood closer to the Pacific, and engaging full-time in the community work I had begun to pursue several years earlier. I continued to organize parties for Jewish singles, and Rabbi Cunin continued to disapprove from a distance.

What finally and formally broke ties was when I announced that actor Richard Dreyfuss would be the guest of honor for my first annual banquet for Chabad of West Los Angeles. Dreyfuss was a controversial choice; he had recently made a trip to Israel during which he met with Palestinian leaders, as well as Israeli officials. Rabbi Cunin ordered that I cancel the gala. Of course, I refused, gave up my formal affiliation with Chabad, and announced the formation of The Chai Center in 1989.

It was perhaps the first time a Chabad rabbi broke away from the movement's hierarchy, stayed in the same city, and opened his own organization. "I am still a Lubavitcher in my heart," I told the Jewish Telegraphic Agency, "but by no longer being an official Chabad representative, I figured I could do even more outrageous things."

Ironically, today there are more than ninety Chabad installations with primary outreach to young adults, said Mayshe Schwartz, who is affiliated with Chabad in Massachusetts. The singles parties that were so controversial in the 1980s are now fully sanctioned under organizational headings such as Chabad Young Professionals. "All they deal with is millennials and singles and young adults, throwing parties at venues and clubs all over every major [American] city," Mayshe said. So, what Schwartzie innovated in the 1980s, he added, "I just see as my father's being ahead of his time by a long shot."

Nor did Schwartzie leave the Lubavitcher sphere by opening The Chai Center. "My father was totally accepted in every circle of Chabad," Mayshe said. "He'd be flown out to Vancouver, to Toronto"—in fact, all over the United States, Europe, and as far as Australia—"and he was in Safed for eighteen summers in a row. Nobody saw the break with Chabad in Los Angeles as a reflection on my father. People just saw it as a political skirmish that ultimately he was on the wrong side of because he was the employee, not the employer. It was just too bad, and we all moved on."

There was one person from whom I did seek approval: the Lubavitcher Rebbe. I was a little concerned how the Rebbe would view this. So, I flew to New York and asked the Rebbe for a blessing "for the formation of my new organization to spread the teachings of Torah." The Rebbe gave me a blessing and then asked that "I put charity in the new charity box in the new organization." That's all I needed to hear from the Rebbe, and I was off and running.

With the establishment of The Chai Center came all the catchphrases I used as come-ons to unaffiliated Jews:

"Don't pay to pray!"

"For Conservative, Reform, and any Jew that moves."

"Come to the shul that doesn't want your money."

"Business is booming!"

And it was: Jews showed up by the score for Shabbat dinner, by the hundreds for parties at venues such as the House of Blues and the Comedy Store and for Passover seders, and by the thousands for Rosh Hashanah and Yom Kippur. Many of them were Jews who hadn't stepped into a synagogue since their own bar and bat mitzvahs, part of the legion I called "Jews for nothing." Los Angeles journalist Tom Tugend summed up the center's outreach strategy succinctly: "Schwartz's unorthodox approach and style [was] based on the simple premise that if Jews, especially the younger generation, won't go to synagogues or join Jewish organizations, then he has to go where they normally gather or provide a setting in which they feel comfortable."

I attracted crowds with a constant offering of varied programs—classes and lecture series and concerts along with the services, dinners, and social events—and an unquenchable drive to go where Jews were and hand out flyers for the programming.

"Shlomo was absolutely a genius in his publicity," Olivia said. "His charisma did the rest. Once they would come in the door and they would meet Shlomo, they would stay. The key was just to get people to come in the door. You have the product, you have what to say, you have what to give them, and there's that warmth and acceptance, but you need to have access to people. So, his creativity was really quite extraordinary in being able to find ways to relate to people and bring them in. That's why he dressed the way he dressed, to make himself approachable and make people interested to find out, 'Who is this person?'"

It also didn't hurt that I had warm relationships with Jewish clergy among the non-Orthodox and Modern Orthodox movements. My willingness to relate to Jews who didn't necessarily adhere to strict Jewish practice also drew people to me.

I was very open in how I looked at things, to not have a pre-formed opinion. I would try to make a connection to see how a person could live with something more Jewish in his or her life than maybe what was being done at that moment. I wanted to open the Jewish doors for people.

Along with the T-shirts and baseball caps, humor was an enormous factor in my outreach. My Purim celebrations at the Comedy Store were as much stand-up as Purim Megillah reading. During a "Stump the Rabbi" session, when a young man asked whether there's a prayer one says before having babies, I replied, "Yes, you pray she doesn't have a headache." David Suissa, publisher of *The Jewish Journal of Greater Los Angeles*, once described my style as one that "no matter how deep the subject, matched his personality: folksy, quirky, joyful." I told another journalist, "Humor is the medium that dispels the misconception that Judaism is uptight and serious."

It all worked. During the years The Chai Center has operated, on a budget comparable to that of a small synagogue, the center's programs have attracted an estimated ten to fifteen thousand people each year.

As The Chai Center got off the ground, I basically kept doing what I had been doing for the past several years: holding massive High Holiday services and seders, throwing parties for hundreds of Jewish singles, presiding over lifecycle events, and teaching. But leaving Chabad gave me an additional, crucial task, one that I hadn't been required to do at UCLA Chabad House: now I had to raise money. And that wasn't my strength.

"He was a terrible fundraiser," Mayshe said. "Couldn't ask, never asked for a penny. A philanthropist, a potential donor would say, 'Hey, Schwartzie, how you doing?' That's his way of saying, 'If you're not doing so well, I'm available for you.' That's the way the communication usually works. But my father never responded with a pitch for money. Someone would say, 'Schwartzie, how you doing?' and he'd say, 'Business is booming. All we're looking for is someone to pay for it.' He'd make like a half-joke, to let people know that we're still on the receiving side.

"But the reality is that once you say business is booming, people will naturally only support where they feel the support is needed. If there's a fire, G-d forbid, they'll support that effort. If there's a famine, they'll support that

cause. If someone says there's no fire, there's no famine, no problem. They move on to the next. So, Schwartzie did not do well in that area, but thank G-d there were enough people over the course of the years who had his back. He had enough fans and support to keep his head above water. He also kept his budget low: he didn't have a big building, did not have a lot of overhead, did not have a personal assistant. He kept things minimal.

"My father was an idealist, so he assumed that when people say they love you, surely that means if they get an envelope in the mail for Passover, they're going to go ahead and put the maximum amount of the options listed," Mayshe said. "I saw that not work with him; I realized that you actually have to have a meeting. You

can't just tell people business is booming. You have to tell them that Jews are booming, but we need X amount."

Once, and only once, Mayshe took Schwartzie on a fundraising mission. "He really was not interested," Mayshe said. "We went to [this one place], and it was not fun. He was uncomfortable as he was sharing his stories. I apologized to him and I said, 'We're never going to do that again. You stay home, you do your thing, and I'll figure it out.'"

Fundamentally, Mayshe said, Schwartzie

"had no patience for externalism or pleasantries or niceties. He did not go to dinners and look for his name tag and find out which table he was supposed to sit at. He worked the room. He went to the people he wanted to say 'hi' to, the people he felt he needed to say 'hi' to, and when he was done, he left. He didn't give in to all the phony niceties that are out there. He didn't have the patience for it.

"He was a direct marketer," Mayshe said. "The ultimate direct marketer."

Chai, of course, is a Hebrew word meaning "life," but it was also an acronym for **C**enter for **H**appiness and **A**wesome **I**nsights. I've been called a Reform Chasid and G-d's court jester, but whatever the label, I do believe that to bring Jews back into the fold, one must serve G-d with joy.

"Schwartzie reaches people no one else can reach because he's so open and tolerant and accepting and embracing," Rabbi Nachum Braverman, education director of the Los Angeles branch of Aish Hatorah, told the Los Angeles Times. "I never met anyone who didn't like Schwartzie."

Ruth Judah, *describing Schwartzie's work in The Chai Center:*

There have been few charities that have been thrilled to meet "any Jew that moves." Rabbi Schwartz wanted to meet them all, and he was jazzed to meet everyone . . . He influenced, supported and entertained Jews who shared his favorite characteristic: a Jewish soul.

It didn't matter whom Schwartzie was meeting: black hat or baseball cap, young or old, famous or immigrant, Schwartzie was the rabbi who would ask which tribe your family came from.

For many, this was a question that took visitors back to roots they had never considered. Then he directed participants to find their local shul, where many families continue their Jewish life today. Is there a synagogue in the city without someone who came through The Chai Center?

Purim party, 1987

Purim party, 1988

Megillah reading wth Mendel the Clown

Schwartzie with Comedy Store owner Mitzi Shore OBM

Schwartzie with Hollywood legend Bruce Vilanch

Purim at the Laugh Factory

Schwartzie receiving a blessing from the Lubavitcher Rebbe for the formation of the Chai Center

Schwartzie offering "Jewish astrology" at Venice Beach

A Jewish astrology reading, based on someone's Hebrew date of birth

Nobody missed me with this garb!

CHAPTER 23

CHAI HOLY DAYS: "DON'T PAY TO PRAY"

The High Holidays, Rosh Hashanah and Yom Kippur, as they are for Jewish congregations everywhere, have been and continue to be the high point of the year for The Chai Center. I saw the holidays as a way to resurrect those Jews who were hanging on by their fingernails, almost lost to their religion. And I figured out early on that the key to attracting Jews who wouldn't be caught dead in a synagogue was to make the holiday services as little as possible like the ones typically carried out in synagogue—and to offer them free of charge.

Along with free admission, Chai Center services contained contemporary and lighthearted elements. Except for the declaration *Sh'ma yisrael* (Hear, O Israel), all the services were in English. Rosh Hashanah eve featured a "Shmooze and Cruise Singles Party," and in the late 1990s, music was provided by the Schwartz Family Tabernacle Choir: my own seven sons. Olivia would hold a study session for women while I headlined the ever-popular "Stump the Rabbi" session, animated by hundreds of people bursting with questions they'd been wanting to ask since age twelve or thirteen.

Welcome to Jewish America's High Holidays (a.k.a. Days of Awe). The holidays used to be called "revolving-door Judaism"—in on Rosh Hashanah and out on Yom Kippur. The good news is that even Jews who do nothing Jewish the whole year—even the most secular, assimilated Jews—at least *think* about being Jewish when Yom Kippur rolls around. Of course, *what* they think is likely to be, "OK, here goes another year that I'm not going to be in temple on Yom Kippur!"

They always have easy excuses, like having to buy the bloody tickets, which so many people resent! Either people don't have the extra $100, $180, $250 for High Holiday tickets, or it isn't on their priority lists. Or, they do have the money, but are incensed by the demand. They find it offensive: an *entrance fee* for a Jew to walk into a Jewish house of worship.

It happens every year at some synagogue: On Yom Kippur, a Jew is denied entry to a shul because he or she doesn't have a ticket. That actually offends so many Jews that they become angry and resentful, and they throw out the baby with the bathwater and stop going, period. I'm also offended. Shuls in Israel don't do that.

You hear it every year: "I shouldn't have to pay to pray! I should be able to go into a synagogue on the High Holidays. And then they hit you up for *more* money while you're sitting there! I refuse to be part of this shameful extortion!"

Or, there are the humbler excuses: "I forgot how to read Hebrew;" "I never learned Hebrew;" and "I don't understand the Hebrew."

And for some people, it's just, "I'm not comfortable in temple and I can't stand those pompous rabbis."

At Chai Center High Holidays, we removed the excuses.

We make the services free!

You don't need tickets; you can just walk in!

We don't have appeals for donations during the services!

We do everything in English!

We're in a nice place with comfy seats, not a temple!

We have a rabbi who does great stand-up comedy!

No more reasons for resentment and anger!

That's the way you get more than a *thousand Jews* (who have not been to a temple in years) to walk into a service on Yom Kippur.

You cannot estimate the value of a person going back to *inspiring* services after not having been for a while. Sometimes the beginning stages of transformation are shocking—and *healing*! Many Jews need that experience now. Nine out of ten times, that experience comes at exactly the crucial time in their lives when they really need it. And sometimes our policy of "Don't Pay to Pray" causes people to drop a bigger check than they would have if we demanded a certain donation.

The truth is that after a while, many Jews really want to come back to services—but they don't know how. The Chai Center has invested heavily in the idea that if you take away all their excuses, they'll come back. And they have, in very large numbers—so large that we made the temples nervous. When we started in 1988, we started getting calls a few weeks before Rosh Hashanah from synagogue rabbis: "Schwartzie, how can you give out free tickets? You're losing business for our synagogue. People aren't going to show up to us!" But don't worry, we became friends.

Every year, I look forward to meeting first-timers at our Un-Orthodox services. We call ourselves Chasidic Reform!

And the Jews have come, in droves.

Rule of thumb: When Jews start to come *early* to an event, you know there's going to be a crowd! I remember one year, the first night of Rosh Hashanah, we were at capacity.

There were no empty seats about an hour into the service; we were standing room only, and it was getting more crowded. Somebody snitched, and the fire marshal appeared. But there's a large lobby, so when someone walked out of the theater, the marshal allowed another person from the lobby to enter the "sanctuary." How comical: the fire marshal controlling Jews at High Holiday services to maintain order.

I was on stage and could see almost everyone: the focus and concentration and participation and *connection* to the participants' roots (read SOUL!).

It was a large rainbow coalition of Jews from all different "denominations" (except Orthodox), and despite their many differences, they were unified by just one factor—they were all MOTs (members of the tribe).

They all felt warmly welcomed and accepted as members of the same religion, period. There was no distinction of how much or little you knew about the religion, or how well you read Hebrew (or didn't), or what you believed in (or didn't), or when was the last time you were in temple (besides funerals and bar/bat mitzvahs).

I particularly felt good about all this great energy from bright, intellectual Jews who hadn't really been exposed to the riches and depth of authentic Judaism.

After the service, our beautiful ushers and usherettes (I hand-pick them) and our large family would thread through the crowd for hours to meet people one on one. The ushers were all instructed to ask them the same questions:

- Is this your first time at our High Holidays?
- How'd you find us?
- Have you ever been to our free "Dinner for 60 Strangers"?

We were thrilled to note a general profile: A large percentage were first-timers (and young, in their twenties and thirties); they found us through the Internet (if you type "free High Holidays" into Google, The Chai Center comes up in the first screen); and they were enthusiastic about the prospect of a free Friday night dinner in West Los Angeles at a private home, with a choice of thirty age-appropriate single Jews whom they'd not known about.

I've always hated competition, so our niche is "outreach to the non-affiliated." Being the innovative shakers and movers we are, we have pioneered aggressive advertising.

The Chai Center was the first to advertise in the Sunday *LA Times* Calendar section (*very* expensive). We were also the first to advertise in that freebie *LA Weekly*.

Of course, we're in *The Jewish Journal* (you can't miss our ad). The reason we're in the *Journal* is that 90 percent of the older *bubbies* and *zaydes* who read the *Journal* will call their adult grandkids (in their twenties and thirties) and yell at them that they MUST go to the free New Year's Eve Shmooze and Cruise Singles Mixer following the Rosh Hashanah service and bring home a Nice Jewish Girl or Boy!

Another creative twist we initiated a while back was to put flyers on the windshields of cars from noon (to get the lunch crowd) through 4 p.m. (to snag shoppers). You might call it "guerrilla advertising." One year, after a few hours of (at my age) strenuous physical exercise (putting flyers on hundreds of cars), I took a break and was sitting outside the Coffee Bean sipping my soy latte and overheard two guys talking. They appeared to be transplanted New York Jews living in Los Angeles who actually *walked* down the street, so they were seeing the flyers on each car, one after another, with the blaring, glaring title:

"FREE! No Tix! No Appeals! No Reservations Necessary!"

After a while, one said to the other, in an unmistakable Brooklyn accent, "No tickets, no appeals? I wouldn't know I was in shul!"

Of course, I ran after them, and they came back and sat and shmoozed with me for a bit while I gave them some of my standard shtick. That High Holidays season we had two more attendees with Brooklyn accents.

For many years, I've had an ongoing argument with my kids. Of course, I've used the Schwartz family dozen as child labor over the years to put the flyers on cars. But the kids insisted that no one ever comes to events just because they find a flyer on the car.

One year, a lovely couple came to High Holidays services, and somehow, out of the hundreds, we actually did meet personally and hit it off.

A year later, I officiated at their wedding. Two years after that, I was the *sandek,* the one who is honored with holding the baby, at the bris of their first child. At the bris, my son Mendel asked the parents, "How'd you find us?"

"We went to a movie on a Saturday night and came out to find a flyer on our car," the new dad said. "At first, I was angry, but then we started reading the flyer—and decided to go."

Not only that, but my son Mendel, who at the time was The Chai Center's director of development (a fancy title for chief fundraiser), met with the parents of the young couple. They were so thrilled about the kids' (and grandkids') new life path that they wrote a check to underwrite our entire expense for the High Holidays for the upcoming year.

I would always badger my Chai Center "members" to go to their phones and call friends or relatives who hadn't been to temple since Aunt Sylvia's funeral or their great-nephew's bar mitzvah.

Believe it or not—they are waiting for your call!

For years, renting a venue for the High Holidays that would seat hundreds of people was a difficult chore. The nicer hotel ballrooms in parts of Los Angeles with large concentrations of Jews were booked by synagogues that couldn't fit their once-a-year congregants into their sanctuaries. The Chai Center was relegated to hotels away from the Jewish center, in downtown Los Angeles or Hollywood or near the airport. Then we had to listen to complaints about the shlep.

But in 2005, The Chai Center had its first of many holiday seasons at the Writers Guild of America's theater in Beverly Hills, a posh 670-seat venue in a much more central part of the Los Angeles basin. The following year I wrote this:

This is the second year that we scored the schmaltzy venue in Beverly Hills. The theater is five-star and just over the top. Both on Rosh Hashanah and Yom Kippur, it was SRO (standing room only), plus we had about two hundred people in the beautiful lobby where the Rosh Hashanah singles mixer took place. Most of them never walked into the actual service, but that's just fine since they were actively engaged in the all-important mitzvah of perpetuating an endangered species: Jews!

In fact, they were joined by a second crowd of people who had gone to other temples because of social or family obligations. What a wonderfully delicious Jewish mob scene! We had *nine* double sheet cakes (that's nine hundred slices of honey cake, and G-d bless the bakery for slicing all nine) that the collective Jewish feeding frenzy inhaled, in about an hour. Thank G-d we had enough wine and apples and honey. One year, the bakery forgot to slice our sheet cakes. That was problematic.

The next day, we were all curious to see what kind of numbers were going to show to hear the *shofar*, the climax of the Rosh Hashanah morning service, on a weekday. The service was called for 11 a.m., and by noon, we had given out the last of our seven hundred prayer books. I was truly shocked and pleasantly overwhelmed that we had drawn that kind of crowd to hear the shofar.

Then we were eight hundred strong at *Kol Nidrei*, and at the end of Yom Kippur, the *Neilah* service, there were still almost six hundred Jews sitting there. It was so moving as to be almost overwhelming. People definitely got into the "closing of the gates," and I was moved to tears several times during that final service.

I love my job!

One year, in 2013 to be exact, I got a very nervous-making message just a few weeks before Rosh Hashanah. With less than a month to go before the High Holidays, the largest event of the entire year, a rabbi's worst nightmare came to pass.

The Writers Guild Theater informed us that although we had hosted our famous free High Holidays services there for the past eight years to a capacity crowd, and we had a contract, the guild was doing construction this year and was thus unable to accommodate us with its venue. I had only one two-letter word in my lexicon for that: OY!

Frantically, we started searching.

We went to some temples that move to big ballrooms in fancy hotels for their High Holidays and asked to use their main sanctuaries. The answer was no.

We then went to some hotels near LAX. Either the price was astronomical or they couldn't give us Yom Kippur because it was on a weekend. I started sweating underneath my untrimmed beard.

One night, after my son and I visited two different families sitting shiva, we went to see another venue that also didn't work out. It was 11:30 p.m., and we were two blocks from my son Mendel's home when we saw a large building that we somehow had never noticed before, with a sign that it was a film studio. We didn't really think G-d was going to make a miracle that was so close and convenient. Although it was late at night, we knocked on the front door.

Inside was a group of laborers animatedly playing cards. But one seemed to have some authority and knew what was going on.

It turned out that the studio was available for our dates, and even though we would have to rent chairs and other items, it was doable! Before signing a contract, we decided to check out the parking situation. After all, in Los Angeles, if there's no parking, it's not going to happen.

Sure enough, all the signs on both sides of the street posted red warnings. Some spaces were only good for one hour; some were only permit parking for residents.

But Mendel didn't give up. He went from office to office to get the parking restrictions removed in that area for the Jewish holidays. Starting from the mayor, he went to County Supervisor Zev Yaroslavsky, to City Councilman Paul Koretz, to a guy named Jay Greenstein in Koretz's office. When Mendel spoke to Mr. Greenstein, pleading to remove the parking restrictions, the first thing Greenstein said was, "Are you related to Schwartzie?"

Decades earlier, he had been a student at Cal State Northridge when I was a campus rabbi there, and he remembered me fondly. Free, unrestricted parking for hundreds of cars on all the side streets around the venue—done.

I love when that happens. The Lord is great!

For more than twenty years, since the opening of The Chai Center, we have been doing High Holidays services the way I wanted to do them, with no senior authority (other than the One we are doing all this for in the first place). Jews come from as far north as Santa Barbara and San Luis Obispo, and from as far east as Palm Springs and San Diego.

Every year, I wonder whether anybody is going to show up, and every year we have a capacity crowd for almost every service. Even when we started at the film studio, on Rosh Hashanah morning, we used every one of the seven hundred folding chairs we had rented and had hundreds more people standing in the back.

The crowds carry over to The Chai Center's Sukkah Party, four days after Yom Kippur. It's truly a delight. The Jews just don't stop coming. We do our best to maintain an active connection with everyone, hoping that people will bring their extended circles to our programs.

Some of our most devoted fans don't know that the Chai in Chai Center is an acronym for Center for Happiness and Awesome Insights. We knew the acronym is accurate because of the things people have said to me after services and events and in emails. Their wonderful accolades have rung in my ears and continually have inspired and motivated me to work harder for the cause I believed in.

The quotes have been truly precious; I couldn't have done a better job even if I had written the script myself.

- "It's my first time at these services and the first time I actually understood the service."

- "A friend recently dragged me to a service in a synagogue. It was in Hebrew, two hours of painful boredom. This was different: funny and spiritual and *up*."

- "I was afraid of the Hebrew, but it wasn't that bad."

- (An oft-repeated phrase) "I learned a lot."

The best is when they would email wanting information about programs, or, even better, complaining that we *don't* have a class on something. Then I knew we won, because even if we don't have it (because we're essentially a mom-and-pop store with three full-time staff members), that person can be referred to some of our many friends in outreach. OK, they're not as funny as I was, but you can learn a lot from them, and some of them are really nice people who can help guide Jews on a path without being pushy. Thus, they get a sense of fulfillment without having to scarf down the whole enchilada, you know, become *shomer* (observant), everything all at once.

So many otherwise really bright people make the same (foolish) mistake: that you either have to go whole hog (swallow the *chazer* in one gulp) or you don't start. Why is it better to do nothing than it is to do something, even if something isn't everything?

Jewish practices are about making connections. You can choose to be either more connected or less connected. You don't have to make any long-term commitment. It's a daily contract, though you can extend it to weekly, monthly, annually, or for a lifetime.

Or, if you don't want to wait for answers to important questions you've had, you could buy me lunch, and I'd go with you anywhere. (Well, anywhere kosher.)

* * *

What do we prepare for when we prepare for the Days of Awe?

If you line up the Jewish calendar with the Gregorian one, Rosh Hashanah, the beginning of the month of *Tishrei*, corresponds to the beginning of the month of Libra. What's the symbol for Libra? A set of ancient scales!

For Jews, those are the scales of divine justice. At the Jewish New Year, those scales begin to weigh our sins against our good behavior. The Heavenly Court reviews our Jewish conduct (or lack thereof) during the past year, and the past year's performance determines what kind of a year we are going to have.

Needless to say, it is essential that we at least show up for our case before the court because, sometimes, if we repent, if we make New Year's resolutions not to perpetuate ethical and spiritual bad habits and promise to incorporate good practices, we can get a divine pronouncement of forgiveness.

That's one of the reasons Torah commands us to hear the shofar: it's a wake-up call!

Do not miss this all-important, once-a-year mitzvah! All you have to do is SHOW UP.

Even if you "have to" work on Rosh Hashanah (*oy!*), you can sneak away for a quickie mitzvah on your lunch break. Come hear only one set of shofar calls (it takes fifteen minutes); then go do whatever. The rest of the year is guaranteed to be different.

This is the month to ask from the all-powerful Creator and Ruler whatever you need or want. Don't miss the great opportunity to have your every request fulfilled.

Everyone can use powerful divine blessings.
Just show up.

For so many years, I went to Schwartzie and Olivia's High Holidays services. Once or twice, I tried other services, after we joined a shul connected to our son's school, but I always came back to Schwartzie because truly I could go more deeply into my prayer and my soul with him. He knew how to make the prayers meaningful and powerful and to give us just the right amount of space to go within.

—Sandra Frankel

I loved Rabbi Shlomo's presence, his stories, his generosity, and his masterful teaching. He could perform like a showbiz giant, presenting to one-thousand-plus people on the High Holidays. I would watch and learn from his unique blend of spiritual outreach; he was one of the best. I learned from the way he opened his home and brought people in with a love that was free from judgment and an enthusiasm that was connected to the highest sources.

—Marcus J. Freed

When I met my wife, I told her about Schwartzie and about his services, and about how it was Orthodox, and we would not sit together. She was adamantly opposed to that. After discussing it for a while, I made her a deal: try it for fifteen minutes, and after fifteen minutes, I'll meet you in the lobby, and if you don't want to stay, we'll leave. Fifteen minutes into the service, I went into the lobby, and she said, "This is the greatest service ever!"

A few months later we got engaged, looked at each other, and said in unison, "Schwartzie!" That's who had to do our ceremony. We loved our meetings with him, and when the service happened, we both laughed when my wife walked under the chuppah and he said with a smile, "This is it!" Of course, everyone loved him and loved the service, and I am honored to have been married by him.

—David Nathan Schwartz

Marquee for High Holidays at the
Henry Fonda Theater, Hollywood,
1996

On the Henry Fonda bimah

147

Listing for Yom Kippur
services, 2004

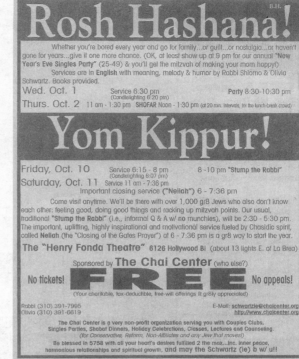

LA Weekly ad for
High Holidays 2006

Welcoming people to
Writers Guild Theater
for High Holidays 2008

Ready for High Holidays at Hi Point Studios on Pico Boulevard , 2013

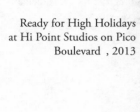

Free Sukkah party

Ad for 1989 Rosh Hashanah services

CHAPTER 24

THOSE WHO KEEP SHABBAT
CALL IT A DELIGHT

The High Holidays were when The Chai Center drew the highest mass numbers, but probably the center's most important function was a regular event with attendance in the tens, not the hundreds. Olivia and I opened our home in Mar Vista most Friday nights to host Shabbat dinner for throngs of Jewish singles (and a smattering of couples) in an event we called "Dinner for 30 Strangers," though the number of Jews crowded around the table ranged up to sixty. We eventually titled these dinners "Dinner for 60 Strangers." These weekly gatherings had one unabashed objective: get more Jews to meet and marry each other.

That's one reason David Suissa of *The Jewish Journal* called me "a one-man Jewish continuity machine."

I would designate some Friday nights for younger folks and others for singles of a certain age, so matches made at the scene would be age-appropriate. Anything else—level of education, earning power, extent of Jewish observance—was irrelevant. And if not every dinner produced a marriage, most of them generated new ways of looking at Jewish tradition and new long-term allegiances and a relationship with The Chai Center.

To further promote these singles dinners, I periodically would send this Chai Center bulletin:

The last two Shabbat dinners for singles were *crowded*!

I guess we finally found what people are looking for:

151

A: An informal, chill atmosphere in a private house

(not an impersonal corporate edifice or temple), expressed via our

B: "Shmooze and Cruise Happy Hour," which is the absolute best ice-breaker, with great body language, in the flow of rooms and outdoor deck of a *home*.

(That's why people do *not* come fashionably late, if they can help it.)

C: A free, delicious, full-course dinner, with amazing homemade gefilte fish, home-baked whole-wheat challah, chicken (or veggie) soup with matzah balls, and so on, and so on.

D: Sitting at the table with thirty choices of the opposite sex within a fifteen-year radius.

E: Schwartzie doing meaningful stand-up between courses, and

F: Olivia telling a moving, tearjerker Chasidic story before dessert.

G: The schmoozing now picks up energy, and the din of conversation rises to a ROAR (till about midnight).

What part of this is not to like?

RSVP ASAP!

The first thirty women and the first thirty men who apply will be admitted!

Nina Rubin was drawn by Schwartzie's deep spirituality and openness to questions.

> *I'm not really religious. I don't respond well to organized religion or judgmental rules to which many faiths subscribe. But this man—this religious, inclusive man—spoke to me on a different level.*
>
> *I met him in Los Angeles around 2005. I was introduced to him and invited to his "Dinner for 60 Strangers." I like dinner. I like meeting people. I was happy to attend.*
>
> *At the dinner, I noticed just how engaging and charismatic he was. I appreciated his wife, who is an excellent cook and baker, and spoke honestly and sincerely. And he had a lot of kids of all ages, and they each seemed very cool.*

This man was deeply spiritual, knowledgeable, and religious. He had an enormous effect on me. We had meandering conversations about my family and the history of how we ended up in our little community in Northern New Mexico. He was open-minded and inclusive. I had previously thought that religious and spiritual folks were judgmental and lived by a stringent set of rules, and that if I didn't play by the same rules, they'd lecture or drop me.

Schwartzie listened to me and got to know me.

He accepted me.

Schwartzie was fair, just, reasonable, and so, so wise. He helped me become proud of myself and of being Jewish. Through some of his teachings, I realized that Judaism doesn't have to be an expensive fashion show in which people pay to pray. It doesn't need to be done in a fancy, gilded building. It just needs to be felt from the heart.

From what I know of Schwartzie, he wanted people to try a little more than yesterday. Of course, he'd strongly encourage and prefer Jews to keep kosher and light Shabbat candles at the proper time on Friday night. But I also know that he was all about asking questions and learning.

Moshe Gellar, like Schwartzie, knew what it was like to be drawn toward both the life of the hipster and the world of strict Jewish tradition.

I got hooked on Schwartzie back in the summer of 1993 by [a mutual friend] who knew what I didn't: my life depended on meeting him. I was hippied out but had returned to keeping Shabbat after four years.

I was living in New York, sort of undercover. After I met Schwartzie and experienced his full-on emes (truth), I couldn't stomach American Jews and Jewishness of almost any kind. There was no place for me within. I was a dyed-in-the-wool Shlomo Chasid. But

that could only be in New York City, when he was in town.

Finally, I got to Los Angeles, and when I arrived at the Schwartz "palace," I knew this was someplace different. Schwartzie was so easy, so "Everything's cool." I told him I would smoke some herb before Shabbat, and he said, "OK. You're an adult; take a walk." And I did. Just not being uptight about the herb told me so much about him and disarmed my protective walls.

He had a million people for the meals. I just observed and took it all in: his amazing-beyond-belief Olivia, his family, the guests. It all touched me deep inside.

By Shabbat morning, it was as if I had been tight friends with Schwartzie and Olivia for years. And so it remained. I only had to keep paying attention to continually learn that no matter how amazing they were, there was always, always, more to see and learn from them.

CHAPTER 25

LIFE CYCLE EVENTS: TRIPLE-HEADER CIRCUMCISION

Wish you were with me at a triple *brit milah*. But it wasn't triplets!

My son-in-law Yakov Shallman conducted a wedding in Northern California a while back for a couple that lives here in Los Angeles, but the family lives up there. The bris of their first child was at their beautiful home in Marina Del Rey. They had a kosher caterer for the sixty people who showed up.

Before the bris, I was talking with the mohel, and it seems that the father, who was in his thirties, had not had a ritual bris as a baby, rather a circumcision by a doctor shortly after he was born. The young father, the mohel, and I all went upstairs just before the baby's bris to do a bris on the father. That just involves taking a drop of blood from you know where. Nothing to it.

In the meantime, the father's brother's wife from Palo Alto, who had come down for the bris and is *very* Jewish (even speaks Hebrew) asked, "Where are all the men going?" Someone quietly said that Peter, the new papa, was getting a bris before his son does.

The sister-in-law said, "Well, his brother Matthew didn't have one either!" So she sent Matt right up there, and he had it done also and took the name Matisyahu. It took three seconds, and no one even jumped.

After the bris on the baby, I put tefillin on some of the people. Everyone had a story.

The biggest honor at a bris is to be the *sandek*, the person who holds the baby during the bris. The parents chose the paternal grandpa, who came with his wife, the *bubbe*, from North Carolina for the *simcha*. When I asked the sandek to wear tefillin on such an auspicious occasion, he not only readily agreed, but shared with me that he had grown up in a quite secular family and actually had never had a bar mitzvah, and this was the first time in his life that he was putting on tefillin. According to the holy Talmud, that's a BFD—a Big Fat Deal!

I then approached the maternal grandpa and asked him when was the last time he had donned tefillin, and without hesitation he boomed out, "1952!"—at his bar mitzvah.

I asked the maternal *bubbe* what her Jewish name was, and she knew that it was Simcha. And that is what this was: a *simchah,* a happy occasion!

Right away, another friend said, "My name is also Simcha." So we took him next for the great mitzvah called, "Wrap the straps."

The family is really quite magnificent, considering its total openness and even enthusiasm for all things Jewish, including losing a drop of blood from the adult male organ to have a real bris.

Even GG (short for great-grandma) got into it, speaking fluent Yiddish with me, even though it had been many decades since she had spoken the language. (There aren't a lot of folks who still speak Yiddish in Marin County, where she lives.) She had amazing energy and a positive attitude, and her vivacious answers to my questions just blew me away. I thought she was about seventy-seven, but she has only 27 years left until the Biblical 120!

One more interesting bit of bashertness concerning this bris: The morning of the bris, I was about to leave the house, and my eye fell upon a little card that has the prayer for a pregnant woman according to authentic Kabbalah.

Well, I thought, it's too late for Kate, the baby's mom, as she's no longer pregnant, but then again, maybe I'll meet a pregnant Jewish woman at the bris. Sure enough, Hilary, the very knowledgeable sister-in-law, was expecting her first child, a boy, in a few months. When she heard that the card was for an easy delivery and a healthy baby, she happily relieved me of it.

And, oh, yeah: my son Mendel teaches a Torah study class in Century City for people in the entertainment business, and that's where he met the parents of the new baby. Guess what they named their son?

Mendel!

End of a Bar Mitzvah Era

It's the end of a glorious family career of bar and bat mitzvahs! The twelfth child, our seventh son, stepped up to the podium. His was the last Schwartz family bar mitzvah; from now on we're working on the grandkids.

Last night, Sunday evening, on the holiday of Rosh Hashanah for the trees (Tu b'Shvat), our Yakov gave the keynote address. He had a lot of really great material because his "other" bar mitzvah was in Israel. He let me see some of his speech. I didn't know he had it in him. He came out of left field, the youngest of the dozen, and wound up being extremely creative.

His thoughts about Los Angeles and about Israel under siege in the holy city of Hebron during riots that included police brutality culminated in a rap song for which he composed the meaningful but humorous lyrics. He additionally had some people perform amazing break-dancing, which he had personally choreographed. Not to be missed!

Yakov was always a little quiet; I guess it's kind of hard to be heard if you're number twelve. But put a mic in his hot little hand and he becomes a giant! I don't know where that comes from.

Truthfully, why shouldn't he be a party animal like all the rest of them? (As long as he has the regulation Jewish strings hanging out of his pants and doesn't take gigs on Friday night, it's kosher.)

CHAPTER 26

LIFE CYCLE EVENTS: SH'MA YISRAEL IN AN RV

In the mid-1990s, before cell phones, Facebook, or other social media, I relied on my answering machine and fax machine to conduct business. My phone number was listed in the Yellow Pages, and I'd get fifty to a hundred calls a day that I would screen and call back as my busy schedule would permit. Often, I would ask people to send me a fax with requests or questions. As luck would have it, The Chai Center came up as one of the first Jewish organizations in the Yellow Pages, which was great for business.

One evening, I was in my office, an upstairs wood-paneled room that runs the length of the house, lined with my entire library of Hebrew and English books. It was midnight, a cold, rainy winter night, and the phone rang twice before the call went to the answering machine—long enough to hear, short enough to ignore. A voice started to record: "Hi, there. I got your name from the Yellow Pages, under synagogue . . . My name is Christina. My grandfather is dying and has been unconscious for ten days; he is on home hospice, and we need a rabbi." Christina is not the most Jewish-sounding name, I thought. This was intriguing enough to answer. I picked up the phone. Christina gave me the rundown again, and I told her I'd be right over.

I went to an unfamiliar neighborhood near Culver City, somewhat downscale and, from its vibe, not exactly little Jerusalem. As I approached the address, I saw an old RV in the driveway. Back then, not many Jews took trips in RVs, so it made me think this wasn't a very Jewish-identifying family.

As I went inside, I didn't see what I believed to be a single Jewish face except that of the man lying in the hospital bed. "This is my grandfather," one woman said. I saw an old man, unconscious, lying in bed and surrounded by a group of extended family, mostly Latino. It was 1 a.m., and the story began to unfold.

Sam, the elderly man, had worked for the U.S. Postal Service for nearly fifty years and lived in this neighborhood with his non-Jewish wife, Maria, all that time. Maria knew Sam was Jewish and had asked Christina, the granddaughter, to call for a rabbi for a Jewish burial. I immediately began asking questions, searching for his Jewish name. The wife said he had cousins in Riverside, and one called him Uncle Shimon. Good, he had a name! I then asked what his father's name was. It was David. Perfect: Shimon ben David.

During my nineteen years working as a campus rabbi at UCLA, I also acted as a chaplain at UCLA Medical Center. I knew that when someone is close to dying, you need to get squarely into the person's face and speak loudly so that he or she can hear you. So, I told Maria and the dozen or so family members, people who may very well have never seen a Jew other than Sam in their lives, that I was going to get in Sam's face and speak very loudly, because when a person is in a coma or otherwise unconscious, you have to yell. They all nodded with silent approval. I told them that I was going to call on his Jewish soul with his Hebrew name and chant a special prayer for the soul of Shimon ben David: Sam, son of David.

I moved extremely close to Sam's bed and yelled into his ear the most important one-liner in the Jewish religion: *Sh'ma yisrael, Adonoy Elokeynu, Adonoy echod*: "Hear, O Israel, the Lord is our G-d, the Lord is One." Sam, lying in bed with his eyes still closed, said in response, *Baruch Shem kavod malchuso l'olam vaed*: "Blessed be the name of His glorious kingdom forever and ever." They were the first words he had spoken since falling unconscious ten days earlier.

It was silent. I turned around and saw twelve heads leaning over me, listening intently. Suddenly, all the people in the room started yelling, "The rabbi made a miracle; the rabbi made a miracle!"

Finally, Maria thanked me for coming, but asked that I not return. "Rabbi, we'll call you when we need you." I called every day for several days, and every day someone would answer the phone and quickly end the call. Finally, on the third day, I called, and once again Christina said she would call me and then hung up the phone. As soon as I hung up, Christina called me back to say that while I had been on the phone with her just moments earlier, Sam had passed away. It felt good to know that Sam died as I was on the phone thinking about him, one soul connected to another.

I was able to convince his wife, Maria, to have a kosher burial for Sam in a Jewish cemetery, telling her that he was born a Jew and should be buried as one. We gathered a minyan to help complete the Jewish funeral ceremony, men who stood up for Sam purely because it was a mitzvah to do so.

Shimon ben David left this world in the highest way.

CHAPTER 27

CHAI CENTER NORTH, EAST, AND ABROAD: ON THE ROAD . . .

Cutbacks? Layoffs? Not for us! Chai Center is everywhere.

I held a *shabbaton* retreat in Santa Rosa, about an hour and a half north of San Francisco. Believe it or not, Santa Rosa is actually more assimilated per Jewish capita than San Francisco is, with an even higher percentage of intermarriage. Not exactly the "Jerusalem of America."

The *shlichim* (emissaries) who ran the local Chabad center were phenomenal: an exquisite young couple with four young, adorable children who had come to this "shtetl" five years earlier. We had forty Jews (none were Orthodox) on Friday night at the free, full-course Shabbat dinner, which was cooked by the young rabbi's wife. The attendees were a potpourri of Jews of various and sundry backgrounds. After one look at the crowd, though I spent another ten minutes eavesdropping on their conversations, I decided not even to take out the Xeroxed text I had prepared.

These were Jews who were hanging on by their fingernails, and this was their last stop (last try/last chance) before complete and total oblivion. To their credit, their non-Jewish spouses were truly curious and thus had come along for the ride.

After the *shabbaton,* the rabbi and his wife emailed me a letter of thanks, telling me that many individuals had come over to them to say that they thought the funny rabbi from Los Angeles had actually talked directly to them Friday night.

On Saturday morning, a different group of twenty-five men and about fifteen women showed up at a storefront synagogue in a mini-mall to daven. After services, everyone stayed for a light Shabbat meal and to shmooze with their own, the observant Jews who are a tiny minority in a large shtetl called Santa Rosa.

Meanwhile, Olivia was in Palm Springs hosting The Chai Center's "For Women Only Spa Retreat," bathing in natural, healing, mineral hot springs while soaking in the mystical spirituality of the South African Kabbalah scholar and master teacher Shimona. (She has a great accent!) It's a little pricey, but after the weekend concludes, no one mentions price again. People are so blown away by the food, the seminars, and the heavenly relaxation that they can't believe they nearly didn't come. Everyone is mentioning the names of dear friends who *absolutely* should have come because it would have *saved* their lives, marriages, relationships, or souls.

* * *

It was nice to know that name recognition of Schwartzie (that'd be me) was spreading beyond California. One weekend, I flew to Boston for three gigs.

Our son, Mayshe, founded Chai Center East in Brookline, Massachusetts, just a few years ago, and thank G-d, business is booming!

Saturday night, he had a "Shmooze and Cruise" happy hour for singles, and instead of the expected thirty, almost one hundred people showed up. I was telling true stories of experiencing the Hand of G-d at Woodstock I and II, and those painfully straight people were *plotzing* loudly. On Sunday night, I was a speaker for a new, progressive Jewish day school in schmaltzy Watertown, and I even got those suit-and-tie people to offer up some belly laughs a few times.

But the crowning glory was the *shabbaton* in Chestnut Hill, which drew about one hundred people. I was definitely "on" that night and spoke three times, with positive results from the crowd. Then, we went around and had one person at each of the ten tables introduce him or herself.

Halfway through the introductions, a renowned physician, well known to the locals, who is also a professor at one of the top medical schools, stood up and smiled at me and told his story. In 1982, he was at UCLA Medical Center and went to my public Passover seder with his wife. He repeated a story I had told at the seder, a story he says changed his life, and that he still thinks about.

Then, a young resident rose and asked me whether I lived near National and Sawtelle Boulevards in Los Angeles. When I gave him a strange look, he said that he was doing a rotation at the Veterans Affairs Hospital in West Los Angeles the previous summer, when I was in Israel with Olivia. One day, he was shopping at Ralphs supermarket, at National and Sawtelle Boulevards, and saw a few young men with kipot and dangling tzitzit in the parking lot.

He asked them whether there was a shul in the area. They said not really, but, as it was Friday afternoon, he should come over to their house for Shabbat dinner. Those young men were our sons, and the young doctor ate in my home for Shabbat dinner—but he didn't realize it was my house until that night in Chestnut Hill, Massachusetts.

I love when that happens!

* * *

From 2009: My son, Mendel, the young patriarch of smuggling Judaism into the bowels of "the industry," which people outside Los Angeles know as the "entertainment industry," had another major hit on new territory. The Cannes Film Festival (yes, the one in France) has enjoyed a tremendously successful run for more than sixty years. We are proud that The Chai Center has become the first (and thus far the only) Jewish organization to arrange a catered kosher Shabbat dinner for "any Jew that moves" who travels to Cannes for the festival. A service precedes the dinner and, amazingly, many *machers* (big shots) come to the Shabbat dinner: almost a hundred people, all told.

This year was the first in which The Chai Center, again under the officiation of Rabbi Mendel Schwartz, had a Shabbat program that included dinner at the Sundance Film Festival in Park City, Utah. About ninety Jews fought in line and nearly came to blows trying to grab seats for the traditional Shabbat foods that many never eat when home in Los Angeles or wherever.

CHAPTER 28

ARE YOU HOMELESS?: A TEENAGER DISCOVERS HER JEWISH IDENTITY

Sara was just seventeen when I met her after Yom Kippur services in 1992. She stayed with other volunteers to help disassemble the rented worship space and box up hundreds of prayer books. She remained at work until everyone but my family members had left, at which point I approached her and asked, "Don't you have anywhere to go? Are you homeless?"

I was closer to the truth than I knew: Sara, already a mother, had been homeless when her daughter was born the previous year, though she had recently found a place in subsidized housing and was receiving state assistance while completing high school.

Sara had grown up speaking Spanish in East Los Angeles, and most of her ethnic background was Mexican. "I grew up with nothing. We were so poor," she said. "You know, I lived with the cockroaches; they didn't live with me. There were eleven of us living in a rundown three-bedroom house." Her mother, born to a Jewish mother but married multiple times to gentiles, was married to an Iranian Muslim when Sara became pregnant at age fifteen. He kicked her out of their house.

After I spoke to her, Sara burst into tears and began to run away. I wasn't going to let her get away, so I ran after her. Thus began a long relationship.

The humor didn't make sense to me because I didn't understand Judaism at the time. I sort of sat close to the front. And I noticed that he kept referring to his wife, so I'm starting to pick up on, OK, that's Olivia, his wife, and these are all his children. And I wanted to meet them.

I stayed throughout the day; I had no idea what I was doing, and I knew nothing about what page we were on or what you're supposed to read. It was very confusing. But I stayed until the end of the day, and they were putting the High Holiday books back in their boxes, taking down the mechitzah; they were packing up, getting ready to go. I thought they needed help, so I started packing up boxes. I just kind of wanted to connect somehow.

Schwartzie asked me, you know, "What are you doing, what's up with you, what are you doing here?" And finally, he asked, "Why are you still here?" And I told him, "This is my first Yom Kippur; I've never been to temple before. I don't know what I'm doing."

Up until then, everything that I had learned about Judaism just seemed very complicated. Like the whole Shabbat thing, not using electricity; I didn't understand it—it was so foreign to me. When you come from absolutely no Judaism at all, it just seems odd; it's weird. And it just seemed so complex, like I don't know what I'm getting myself into, and I want to know more, but is this really for me? But after I heard Schwartzie speak, I really knew, this is whom I want to learn from. This is the person I want to teach me about Judaism. I can understand him. If he breaks it down for me, I get it.

And I started to. Everything he said— of course not on the first day—but he just started making so much sense to me. He kind of took me under his wing and started sending me to different houses for Shabbat dinner.

Judaism is what finally made sense to me. I finally felt like I belonged somewhere. I finally felt like I had an identity. It didn't happen right away. But just growing with him and his guiding me . . . anytime I had a question, anytime I had something that was stressing me out, I knew that I could call him and that he would be there for me. He eventually helped me get my daughter into a Hebrew day school. He got somebody to sponsor her. I had a son, a second child, when I was twenty-two, and he sponsored the bris because I was still on government aid at the time. He set it up; I didn't have to do anything. He made all the arrangements with Chabad of Pasadena. My son would not have had a bris otherwise.

And he was the only person who was there for me. I didn't have family to speak of. My mom is totally anti-Jewish. My dad is Muslim. He berates Judaism regularly. He continues to tell me how my mom's such a dirty Jew. Stuff like that. So I didn't have family to turn to. Whenever I had anything really serious going on in my life, Schwartzie was the only person I could talk to. And I could talk to him about anything. He never made me feel uncomfortable about being a teenage mom.

At one point, I moved into Pico-Robertson, which is a Jewish neighborhood, and I felt quite ostracized. I was the odd man out, definitely. Except for when I was with Schwartzie. And so I kind of felt connected to Judaism through him because I understood him. I got him. He made sense to me.

And he did that for a lot of people.

There's a story about his meeting my grandmother, right before my son's bris. My grandmother had not spoken Yiddish for thirty years, or something like that. And he walked into her hospital room—she was dying—he walked into her hospital room and started speaking to her in Yiddish, and she responded to him! She died the next day, and he officiated at her funeral.

When my daughter had her bat mitzvah, Schwartzie and I happened to be in Israel at the same time, and he did a bat mitzvah ceremony at the Wall with her. I cannot say enough about him. I want to say so much about him, because there's no one who made me feel better about who I am than he did.

I met Schwartzie at the perfect time. It was synchronicity, one of his favorite words.

LOVE, MARRIAGE, AND *BASHERT*

CHAPTER 29

THE WEDDING OF G-D AND THE JEWISH PEOPLE: SHAVUOT AS METAPHOR

I would often brag about the hundreds of weddings at which I had officiated, and it is an impressive total. Even over a career of more than forty-five years, eight hundred weddings is pretty extraordinary. And many of these couples are still married. No doubt, it was the lifecycle event of weddings that gave me the most satisfaction, because I saw a wedding as not only the bringing together of a loving couple and the creation of a new Jewish home, but also as the reenactment, again and again, of Judaism's first defining moment.

The holiday of Shavuot always comes fifty days after Passover because it commemorates the event that began the Jewish religion, namely, the receiving of the Torah at Mt. Sinai. Seven weeks after we were liberated from slavery in Egypt, we were all standing at the foot of Mt. Sinai, listening to the Almighty's voice boom out, "I, the Lord, am your G-d who brought you out of the land of Egypt . . ." Great experience!

However, what does that mean to anyone today? What is the practical value of remembering that event from more than three thousand years ago? In general, what's the most popular image that captures everyone's attention?

Romance—a loving couple.

That's why when Kabbalah teaches about getting close to G-d, it uses detailed sexual imagery. Did you know that? It explains that when there are two opposites, like X and Y chromosomes, or a finite being and an infinite being, how do we harmonize them?

It does it by borrowing the image of a man and woman essentially in unity—two who are joyfully coming together as one. But when does that begin? Obviously, at the wedding.

What does the Talmud say about the great theophany, G-d's dramatic giving of the Law to the Israelites? It calls that event the wedding between the groom (that would be G-d) and the bride (that would be us, the Jews). The Torah was the *ketubah* (marriage contract), and Mt. Sinai was the *chuppah*.

Why was the union between G-d and the Jewish people different from all others? Because that marriage was preceded by a prenuptial agreement. The Talmud, in Tractate *Kiddushin*, prohibits a certain precondition to a marriage; the rabbis declared that such a precondition renders a wedding conducted after the events at Mt. Sinai invalid.

What's that condition?

If a man says to a woman, "Marry me on the condition that we will never divorce," that makes the wedding ceremony not kosher!

But that was what happened at our marital union with *HaShem*. He said, "I will never exchange you for another." Isn't that romantic? No matter what happens, regardless of any negative speech or action between the two of us, G-d said at Sinai, we will be eternally connected as one. That's a love match forever!

So, when the Ten Commandments were divinely verbalized for all time, this was our wedding. And the great thing is, we get to relive that wedding every year, on the sixth day of the month of Sivan. People think of the theophany at Sinai as a one-time-only happening, but because that singular event was the all-encompassing birth of the Jewish religion, we reenact it on Shavuot. That translates to each one of us having that actual monumental experience annually on the sixth of Sivan during the reading of the Ten Commandments from the Torah.

Are you ready for that?

CHAPTER 30

THREE WEDDINGS

Every wedding at which I officiated was unique, but some were more unusual than others.

It was the day before Labor Day, and it was 110 degrees in the San Fernando Valley. As luck (bashert?) would have it, I had a big wedding to do at a large, extravagant venue. The names of the bride and groom were Christina Hannafin and Chris O'Reiley; the last names came from his pop and hers, but their moms were both Jewish.

Somehow I got this gig.

Usually, to disarm the Jews when they are surprised to see what appears to be a very Orthodox rabbi with a long, gray beard, I first attack the elders with white hair and start speaking in the vernacular, for example, Yiddish, with a few core phrases that, even if you don't understand Yiddish, you would know because you've heard them so many times from your *zayde* or your *bubbe* or other relatives of a certain age.

I bombed each time. Accordingly, I took a step back and started just belting out "Mazel tov!" People responded with blank stares. There were very few Jews in attendance altogether. But the families and all attendees were extremely respectful of the rabbi and very accommodating. (I like when that happens.)

This high-end venue didn't allow outside food to be brought in, like airline-type meals or food from Pat's Restaurant (a kosher restaurant that caters outside events), which is what we usually do. Everyone feels better

rabbi is staying for the banquet and eating because he has his own
.are.

So, they brought me and my other "kosher" witness a large picnic
cooler with a dozen pieces of pita, a bag of Israeli cookies, and a package of
sliced kosher turkey.

The punch line here is that Christina, who is a quite successful young
executive, went to the mikvah and had an amazing, cathartic spiritual
experience.

And Chris put on tefillin with me, just before he went to the chuppah,
and told me that he felt strong energy reverberating and ricocheting in
him throughout the ritual, something he was quite unfamiliar with. After
wrapping tefillin, he volunteered that he and Christina wanted to come to
our service on Yom Kippur.

It was difficult not being able to play Jewish Geography as an easy ice-
breaker with all the gentiles at the wedding. But Chris's mom and stepdad
live in Brookline, where our son, Mayshe, had just bought a building to
house The Chai Center East.

* * *

I officiated a wedding for a wonderful young Jewish couple who met
in college at UC Berkeley. They were both "Deadheads" and wanted to have
a more-or-less organic event at an outdoor venue rather than a traditional
ceremony. The happy couple was thinking of something like Golden Gate
Park, with the attendees throwing bread to the ducks at the auspicious,
crucial moments. For the reception, guests would just bring potluck (with
non-kosher accepted).

However, the parents of both students were wealthy Orthodox Jews,
and all the grandparents were concentration camp survivors. A compro-
mise was thus struck.

The couple would hire an Orthodox or Chasidic rabbi who was also a
Deadhead, or at least was willing to incorporate some Grateful Dead lyrics
into the ceremony under the chuppah. I'm not an expert—unfortunately
I had only attended six shows before Jerry Garcia died—but thank G-d,
I remembered that in "Scarlet Begonias" there's a Chasidic line that posi-
tively hits the nail on the head.

Armed with buttons pinned to our shirts that said "Jews for Jerry," we
stormed the stage and took up positions that made us look as if we were in
charge. At the opportune moment, I was able to dramatically deliver the
line of that evening:

Once in a while you get shown the light
In the strangest of places if you look at it right.

*   *   *

And, of course, I was over the moon in 2015, when my first grand-child became engaged to a delightful Chabadnik from Brazil.

By now, most of our devoted fans know that we pumped out a dozen kids—five daughters and seven sons, thank G-d. Our oldest son, Shaya, married to Raizy, has nine kids; our next son in Boston has eight; and, thank G-d, nine of our children are married. (We are especially thankful to the Almighty that, so far, all nine married Jews.) There is a Jewish superstition that you don't count grandchildren. But suffice it to say that we are approaching fifty *ayniklach* (Yiddish for grandkids).

And then the first of my grandkids got engaged (to a Jew). This started a new chapter in our family history.

There is a Jewish folk saying: "Who is a Jew? Whoever has Jewish grandchildren!" Just meditate on that for a few moments. It means that if you kept the faith strong enough that your children made sure their kids (your grandchildren) married Jews, that kind of validates you as a Jew—someone who isn't breaking but rather keeping the chain of four thousand years and counting.

I have to thank our granddaughter, Shula, for "making me a Jew."

The boy is from Brazil, and he actually has translated, so far, twenty volumes of the Rebbe's Torah talks into Portuguese. He's quite a good-looking guy, by any and all standards, a good match for our nineteen-year-old Shula, who is definitely a show-stopper. (If she dressed like most young women of today, she would cause car accidents.)

The wedding was in the Holy Land, a.k.a. Brooklyn. We all blessed the couple to get married at the most auspicious time of divine favor, and may it be an eternal, everlasting edifice according to the laws of Moses.

Somehow, I never thought that the Almighty would grant me such a precious gift as being in attendance, in the flesh, at the historic, momentous occasion of the first Schwartz grandchild's wedding!!!

I have spent my adult life not just happy, but in ecstasy—thankful, appreciative, and extremely grateful (although undeserving) for the divine lovingkindness of the absolutely greatest present a human can be granted by the Creator: the gift of being alive!

Especially when the Benevolent One has so many of our loved ones involved in family *simchahs*, through His divine medium called synchronicity (bashert in Yiddish).

Sandra Frankel was part of Schwartzie's circle in Los Angeles.

A dear friend, after giving me the thumbs-up of approval for Gadi, the Israeli man I was dating, gave me Schwartzie's phone number when we arrived at the point of discussing marriage. She said, "Here's the rabbi for you!"

Meeting him was such a delight that it still makes me smile. He had a list of questions to get through to make sure our marriage would be kosher. He was all business, but with such a loving and joyful heart.

Then he invited us to have Shabbat with his family. It was a requirement more than an invitation. I'll never forget that Shabbat. Olivia's hummus was seriously heavy on the garlic; there were lots of kids, singing . . . I just took in the love of this incredible family, particularly the way the women were honored, so unlike my own family. I felt something new take hold in my heart.

Being married by a rabbi of Schwartzie's spiritual stature was an honor I can never express. He brought something truly mystical to our ceremony, and I know the magic of that night under the chuppah has seen us through and helped our love to grow beyond what I ever could have imagined.

Just a few of Schwartzie's 800-plus weddings!

CHAPTER 31

JUNG AND SYNCHRONICITY: THERE ARE NO COINCIDENCES

It was psychologist C. G. Jung who coined the term "synchronicity" in the 1920s to label events as "meaningful coincidences." Something that seems amazing happens, and it feels as if it *had* to happen because it connects directly to something you'd just been thinking about, or something you were involved with, or somewhere you lived a long time ago.

It's the hoped-for outcome of every game of Jewish Geography: "Who'd have thought I'd go to my wife's fortieth college reunion and meet someone I went to summer camp with? AND he's friends with my cousin Shelly!"

Of course, Jewish tradition was all over that concept, also known as "destiny" or "fate," long before Jung got hold of it. We know it as *bashert*.

To me, bashert experiences were as common—and as delicious—as a toasted bagel with cream cheese and a nice piece of fish. A person who got around to as many places and met as many people as I did was bound to keep running into folks I'd married, taught, prayed with, or hosted for dinner—plus their kids and grandchildren.

I saw the divine hand in almost every chance meeting, but He was really attuned to the events in which you could almost see G-d nodding in approval next to your right shoulder. I considered bashert experiences to be ways of bringing order to a chaotic world. Every time a synchronistic occurrence smacks you in the face—in other words, confronts you directly and undeniably—it invariably points to the fact there is a method to the (seeming) madness in our personal lives.

Those who do not want to change any details in their weekly practice of life usually try to slough off the concept with some cheap cop-out, such as, "It's a small world." But sometimes it's just too far-fetched to use these lame one-liners, which take the pressure off us to change anything. When we truly examine things, it's possible to begin to entertain the idea that perhaps there is a Divine Master Plan . . . The really difficult part is that this implies not only that G-d exists, but also that He participates in our lives.

Bashert moments excited me so much that our weekly Chai e-blasts to our five thousand subscribers were filled with them, usually followed by the exclamation:

"I luv when that happens!"

One such bashertness is about a trip to Montreal for Passover, just after a grandson's birth: our oldest son, living in Brooklyn, had his seventh child (a fifth son) three days before Passover. Because there was no way the new mom was going to cook the meals of the Passover holiday for the family, they packed the three-day-old infant into the family vehicle, along with the other six children, and drove nine hours to her sister's house in Montreal. That meant that if the *zayde* (the grandpa—that'd be me) wanted to attend the bris, I would have to fly to Montreal.

The night after the bris, I had yahrzeit for my mother, may she rest in peace, and needed to buy a memorial candle. My son (the new papa) took me to the Canadian version of Ralphs, simply called IGA.

By "accident," at the check-out line in front of me was a nice-looking, tall, slim Jewish man, about thirty-nine. We started talking and quickly progressed to his having a sister in Los Angeles. Then he asked me, "Do you know a rabbi there named Schwartzie?" My son, standing behind me, started to sputter, "I can't believe this!" I told our new friend, "I am quite close to your sister's brother-in-law, and that's where we stay when we're in Miami. I know your sister came back home, here to Montreal, to be with the family, and we were actually looking to make contact with them here."

After some warm hugs to cement our new/old friendship, I gave him my card, and he promised to give his sister my fondest Pesach blessings.

Three hours later, I got a text message that their father had been admitted to the ICU in a hospital nearby in Montreal. The new papa took me straight to the hospital, and the older man was just coming out of his situation, being downgraded from ICU to a regular room. The joy his daughter exhibited when we walked into that room was only eclipsed by the man's putting his hand on his bare head and reciting prayers that he knew by heart with us.

IT'S NOT A SMALL WORLD!!!

There is a method to the madness—it's called *"BASHERT."*

I luv when that happens!

And some of these bashert stories reach back before I even existed and continue until today.

One day, I met a guy at a wedding just outside of Jerusalem who, like me, had been born in Atlantic City, the town my parents settled in after fleeing Austria in 1939.

Of about three hundred attendees at the wedding, almost all the men wore black hats (instead of just a kipah). Only two people (smart, as it was hot in the Middle East that day) wore white straw hats. One of them came over to me. He looked about my age. I saw by his look that he didn't know me but wanted to engage. He asked me where I had bought my white straw hat with the stylish black band.

We thus started playing my all-time favorite game: Jewish Geography. That's when two Jews who are strangers start talking to each other until they find out they are relatives (or close).

Atlantic City was actually quite a small town of only thirty thousand people, with one hospital. To my query of where in the United States he was from, he answered Jersey. At this point, I realized that another G-dly synchronicity was in the making. Turns out that he is one year older than I and was also born in Atlantic City Hospital and raised in Atlantic City.

My father, of blessed memory, was a cantor there in the Chelsea Hebrew Congregation. That means that my father was a cantor during the war years in Atlantic City . . . The U.S. Army had a base in AC from which the army would ship out troops to the European battlefield. Every year of the early '40s, my father told me with special pride, he would conduct High Holy Days services for literally hundreds of Jewish GIs during Rosh Hashanah and Yom Kippur at the largest indoor auditorium in the United States, the world-famous Convention Hall.

Of course, I related that fact to my new best friend with the stylish white straw hat, born a year earlier in the same hospital as I was.

My dad was the cantor, but I never even asked my dad who the rabbi at those High Holy Days services was. You guessed right! It was my new friend's father.

I just LUV when that happens.

Shira Jacobson was part of the Schwartz "family" from childhood.

I was twelve years old when I first learned the word "synchronicity."

It was Friday afternoon, and the Schwartz house smelled of Olivia's famous freshly baked whole-wheat challah and endless piles of gourmet food bubbling over on the stovetop . . . I felt myself being magnetically pulled toward an enchanting poster of two identical dolphins, jumping out of the sea in perfect symmetry above a long, hard-to-pronounce word I had never seen before.

I tried to read the daunting word out loud: "SEEN-CHHHHHHH-RO-NIS-CITY."

A roaring, deep belly laugh shook the walls of the room. Schwartzie swiveled around his office chair with a big smile on his face.

"Synchronicity—it's my favorite word . . ."

"What does it mean, Rabbi Schwartzie?"

"Has something ever happened to you where you're just completely shocked and say, 'WOW, what a crazy coincidence!' Well, another word for that situation would be synchronicity.

"People sometimes forget that everything in this world is carefully coordinated and planned in advance by the Big Guy Upstairs. Every moment you have gone through, and WILL go through, in your life has purpose and meaning. Even if you THINK it's a small, insignificant experience, it's really not. Each tiny second of life has been planned with much more detail than you could ever imagine."

Every single person you meet, even if it's for a few short minutes, has been deliberately put in your path for a reason. You have something to teach every person you meet, and you have something to learn from every person as well. Rabbi Schwartzie saw divine purpose within each of the millions of people he met and uplifted every engagement, no matter how seemingly insignificant, by pulling the reins of the interactions to focus on G-dly light with sincere compassion.

CHAPTER 32

I LUV WHEN LOVE HAPPENS!

Vignettes of Matches Made

A few years ago, there was a big sports game on the Friday night we were having a huge singles dinner. A good-looking fellow had come from Redondo Beach and got lucky with traffic on the 405 freeway, so he got to our neighborhood in West Los Angeles a bit early.

Having an extra half-hour, he stopped into a bar, a country-western watering hole, to watch the game. After a short while, an adorable woman in stylish, high-heeled cowboy boots and matching hat sidled over to begin the process of his buying her a drink. Almost immediately, he found out that this cutie was *Jewish*.

He explained that he had to go to a rabbi's house soon, even though he wasn't really a practicing Jew, because there was a social mixer for Jews there.

Her face fell. If this was the kind of guy who attends those functions, then she was also ready to attend, but she wasn't exactly dressed for the occasion, with her extremely tight micro-mini jean skirt.

He got to our home a little early and told my wife the story. She kicked him out, saying, "Don't come back without her!"

He returned a bit later with our heroine. Initially, she was shy, but then she began to hit it off with another guy I didn't know, as this was his first time. Eventually, everyone sat down at the six long tables. I noticed she and the new guy sat together.

After a few courses, all the guests took a turn saying their names aloud and how they got to our home. When it came her turn, the woman in cowboy boots actually did a great job telling her story.

Then her new friend, whom she was sitting next to (not the guy who brought her), said his name and that he had just moved to Los Angeles from Texas. At that point, our heroine jumped up and said she was also newly here from Texas, and for the past three months, her cousin from Dallas had been telling her about this great guy who had just moved to Los Angeles and that they should hook up.

I LUV when that happens!!!

Another bashert moment occurred at The Chai Center's "Not a Christmas Party," thrown every December for secular Jews in Southern California. This one happened in spite of Olivia and me:

Among the cheerful throngs at this party, I saw a woman dressed differently. Then I realized that she was dressed attractively but modestly, like an Orthodox *rebbitzen* would be. Then I looked more closely and saw that she was wearing a wig, meaning that she had been married and was now divorced. That did it: she was too religious for the room.

I took her aside and said that this group really was not appropriate for her, and instead of wasting her time, she could do better in a "shul wig" competition or maybe a gefilte fish cook-off. I explained that there was likely no one even remotely connected to what she was obviously very involved in.

Unbeknownst to me, my wife saw a nice-looking man, but he was wearing a kipah and had the white strings sticking out of his pants and a beard, the whole Orthodox shmear, and she told him the exact *same thing*.

Neither of them listened, and then they met each other. A number of years later, after they had kids of their own who blended with her kids into the Chasidic Brady Bunch, her eldest daughter married *our son*.

Bashert means you never know what the Almighty has in store for you!

CHAPTER 33

BASHERT *BA'ARETZ* (SYNCHRONICITY IN THE LAND OF ISRAEL)

As far as I was concerned, there was no place like Israel, my summer home for twenty years, for playing Jewish Geography and experiencing other forms of synchronicity.

There's a verse in the Hebrew Bible that states, "Israel is a land that the eyes of G-d are upon, the entire year" (Deuteronomy 11:12).

Wait a minute—aren't the eyes of G-d on Los Angeles, even Las Vegas, that is, on *all* lands the entire year as well?

It means that Divine Providence (a.k.a. synchronicity, or bashertness) happens in the Jewish homeland way more than it does in Los Angeles (or wherever).

In the old part of Safed, there is a little town square with four small restaurants. Three of the four serve falafel. Sooner or later, you have to pass through the square. There are about twenty small tables with tons of chairs, always full of people doing what I love: hanging out and playing my favorite game, Jewish Geography. Strangers bond incredibly quickly in this singular spot.

I was gobbling down a great falafel plate with fresh-baked whole-wheat pita bread, and I heard a familiar exclamation: "Schwartzie!" Now, who might that be?

About thirty years earlier, in Los Angeles, I got a call about something of an aggravated domestic situation, and the family wanted a rabbi to make a house call. The family lived in Westwood, where I lived at that time. I got there, and there were only two people, neither of whom looked terribly happy.

She had advanced multiple sclerosis and was already in a wheelchair, and her only child, a twenty-five-year-old son named John, was living with her and trying to be something of a caregiver. The husband had been an exercise buff, in great physical shape, who had divorced and left her a few years earlier. They were a typical LA Jewish family belonging to the largest Jewish group in town, "Jews for Nothing."

But now they realized that perhaps they could benefit from something nonphysical, as the realm of the physical looked pretty bleak and wasn't offering much hope or direction. First, we had a conversation, during which I convinced them that a rabbi is pretty much like most nice, normal people and is nonjudgmental. Then I whipped out my tefillin and strapped up her son, who had never performed the mitzvah or, for that matter, even seen a pair of tefillin in his life. They had never belonged to a synagogue, never attended High Holiday services, and he had never been bar mitzvahed nor had any type of Jewish education.

The son started becoming interested in the religion he'd been born into but knew nada about. Zilch.

On the other side of the world, in Lebanon, a Jewish girl got on her motorcycle and escaped the severe anti-Semitism in her country by riding to Israel. Eventually, she arrived in Los Angeles and met John.

I married them in a small ceremony and officiated at the bris of their two sons. The two boys grew up and were put in charge of a yeshiva in Safed for spiritually inclined Jews.

Those two fellows were the ones who called to me in the square in the ancient city of Safed.

* * *

Long ago, I performed a small wedding in Los Angeles in a neighbor's backyard. Both were Israelis. We grew close, and the guy became one of my drinking partners.

They had a son and a daughter. I was the *sandek* for the boy. When the girl grew up, I officiated at her wedding—my first second-generation wedding.

Years later, Olivia and I were once again scholars-in-residence at the Ascent Institute in Safed. Many people came through during the summer, so Ascent looked for a young, rabbinical couple to be employed as junior scholars-in-residence to answer questions, teach classes, and so on.

And who got the job? It was the little boy whose parents I had married and whom I had held when he was eight days old at his bris. A week ago, he and his wife just walked in the door, and we were so happy to see them! Then they told us that they were now our coworkers.

Wait, that was just for starters!

I taught a minimum of two classes a day called "Kabbalah for Dummies," a.k.a. "Advanced Mysticism for the Beginner."

One morning, two new people came to my class: one older (about my age), quite Orthodox, with a white beard, and a young twenty-something. They both had heavy Southern accents.

Almost every class had new people attending, so before each class, we would go around to introduce ourselves, say where we are from, and describe how we arrived at this off-the-beaten-track small town of Jewish mysticism called Safed.

The older man was shy and spoke very little, except to say that he had made aliyah a few years earlier and was from North Carolina. The twenty-something gave his Hebrew name and said that he was also from North Carolina, but from a shtetl that no one had ever heard of because it was so small that it only had one stop light. The older man perked up and asked him the name of the shtetl. When the younger man said "Greenville," the older guy jumped up and called the fellow by his American name, and they both recognized each other and embraced!

I'm not finished.

When we got to Safed one year, there was a new, young married staffer who was Israeli-born and was teaching in the Hebrew-speaking part of Ascent.

I soon realized that he spoke fluent English and began asking him about his background. He told me that his parents had been born in the States. Then he surprised me by asking a question that I heard more frequently the older I became: "Are you Schwartzie?"

He told me that his mother met me when she was a student at UCLA and I was a campus rabbi there, back in 1972, and I started her off on a journey that culminated in her making aliyah, and he's the result.

I love when that happens!

Of course, it didn't have to be Safed. I could be sitting pretty much anywhere in Israel, and soon someone from my past would come by.

I was sitting in the Old City of Jerusalem at a great little funky cafe, having a delicious cappuccino with a friend from Los Angeles who had moved to Israel about six years earlier.

When I first met him and got to know him a little and found out that at age forty-seven he had never put on tefillin, I took him out of the category of Jews who had never had that experience. Years later, he had progressed to a level of beginning to practice his religion a little more and going to Torah study classes and the like.

The woman I introduced him to had "too much makeup," but thank G-d, he found his soulmate, a lovely Jewish woman, and they moved to Tel Aviv. In the outreach trade, we call that going from zero to one hundred! Now he is full-blown Orthodox. That can happen even in the nicest of families. I don't know whether he'd eat in my home anymore, as it might not be kosher enough!

My now religious-fanatic jihadist friend challenged me: "But do all your efforts ever produce *real* Jews?" I respond that all people born of Jewish mothers are *real* Jews, even if they are members of the largest group of Jews, the ones I call "Jews for Nothing."

Then a pretty young woman passed by with a tiny baby in a carriage. My friend greeted her warmly and was about to introduce her to me, but she smiled at me knowingly and said, "Steve and I met at a Chai Center Rosh Hashanah service at a hotel near LAX when neither of us was involved in the religion, and after Schwartzie did his stand-up routine, we started going to his home for Shabbat dinners on Friday nights." Then she said to me, "Our five kids are your 'grandkids!'"

Two minutes after she had left, an ultra-Orthodox-looking man, complete with beard and the standard "penguin" outfit (black suit, white shirt, black fedora) came over to our table and said to me, "You don't recognize me, do you?" (Over the last thirty-six years in my profession, that happened more and more frequently, but it's still embarrassing.)

He said his name used to be Louis when he lived in Santa Barbara, but he exchanged that name for Eliezer. He was living in a suburb of Jerusalem and had seven children! It is so great to find out about all these extra grandkids!

Then someone else came over and said that tonight there would be a Torah study class being given in Jerusalem by a recognized young scholar who is also a well-known musician, a guy named Yakov.

In Los Angeles, I knew him as Jon.

The first time he came to our home for Friday night dinner, I asked him whether he wouldn't mind changing his T-shirt for a shirt of mine. He was then performing in the musical *Jesus Christ Superstar* and was proudly sporting a T-shirt from the production.

He was actually a bit offended that I would ask him to change. I gently explained that it was actually a first for me; until that time, I had never asked anyone to change his attire. But it was uncomfortable for me to conduct a Shabbat dinner with that bold, in-your-face message (made bolder by Jon's being a big, tall guy).

He is now one of the top musicians in Israel (no more JC T-shirts) and married to an absolutely lovely Jewish woman who had been in a cult for almost ten years. They have more of my "grandkids."

There are no accidents! It is *not* a small world! Things happen and are synchronized by divine detailed supervision and intervention.

And so it goes in G-d's country.

CHAPTER 34

BASHERT: CAPE COD AND UBER

I was always on the lookout not only for straying Jews, but for "stray" Jews: people whose Jewish connections had frayed not by their own choice, but by circumstances of family or geography. I found one such stray on the beach at Cape Cod after leading a retreat weekend.

Early Sunday afternoon, when 95 percent of the people were gone, Olivia and I finally had some "alone" time. People took us up on our offer to answer any question, so we had hours of, "I've had this question forever and never got a satisfactory answer from any other rabbi . . ."

At long last, we were strolling along the beach. It was chilly and windy, but the ocean was calm, and there were only about three and a half people on the beach.

An elderly woman was walking her tiny dog. I can tell from two blocks away if someone is Jewish—or isn't. She was not.

But Olivia started talking to her, and she stopped and looked us over closely and then said, "I live here. Is there a temple around here?"

Then she began her story. Her mother had converted to Catholicism (*oy!*) to keep the peace when she married her Italian Catholic father, and they had sent her to Catholic school. "But I always knew," she whispered to us, "that in my heart of hearts I remained a Jew."

When her mother died, a few years after her father, she told her brother that she wanted to hire a rabbi to officiate at her mother's funeral and recite the Kaddish. "Am I saying that right?" she asked us. She was.

The next morning, when she got to the funeral, her brother told her that he had already fired the rabbi, who had told him brusquely that he had another gig and could only stay five minutes after the funeral, and he could not go back to the house—and, by the way, his fee was $250. (My mother, of blessed memory, told me that my *zayde* used to say, "Present-day rabbis are leading the Jews—to become apostates and convert out!")

Olivia probed further, and the elderly woman told us that she remembered her mother's mother lighting Shabbat candles!

Then she said that she had a thirty-two-year-old son who lives in Manhattan and is secretly seeing an absolutely lovely woman from an Orthodox family, but she won't tell her parents because she thinks the son isn't Jewish. So we told her the good news: that we are Chasidic and wholeheartedly endorse the union!

Thus, almost three generations of Italian-Catholic lost Jews are getting another chance because of a (bashert) stroll on the beach at the Cape.

* * *

After a car accident, I quit driving and was almost a shut-in before Uber came along. Hundreds of drivers later, I was ready to fit Uber into my unified theory of bashertness.

When do we see G-d?

How do we experience G-d?

Where are those biblical miracles that used to happen so frequently?

If only I could see a few spectacular miracles!

But nowadays, divine intervention (a.k.a. a miracle) takes a slightly different form.

In Spanish, it's called *destino*.

In Hebrew, *hashgachah*.

In Farsi, *ghesmat* (that's kismet to you!).

In Yiddish, *bashert*.

In English, divine providence, or my favorite word, synchronicity!

It's one of the main topics of Jewish mysticism (Kabbalah).

How to see G-d and achieve a mystical union with G-d is the goal of true religion.

The above is an important lead-in to my experience with more than five hundred Uber drivers. I haven't been around that many gentiles since being beaten up in public school. I've learned a lot.

I try to talk to each one about belief in one G-d and about the Middle East. I have better luck with G-d than with the Middle East. Many of the drivers are believers in a specific religion or lapsed Catholics who go to church only on Christmas and Easter (kind of like our assimilated Jews who only go to temple on Rosh Hashanah and Yom Kippur). One Christian driver was complaining about the Catholics, that they're too extreme. It reminded me of our people complaining about the ultra-Orthodox and their "extremism."

When my smartphone told me that Boris would be my Uber driver, I knew where he was from. I only speak three languages fluently, but I know about ten words in another nine languages. As it happens, I have a great accent, so the people to whom I say a few words in one of those nine languages (including their indigenous slang) start talking to me a mile a minute and don't believe that I actually do not speak their language.

Boris arrived, and I got in and greeted him in flawless Russian for close to two sentences. He lit up like a light bulb, and for another long paragraph, he rattled away in the tongue of Mother Russia.

Then I got him back to reality concerning my language skills. Of course, I had my Jewish antennae out and working. I could see that he wasn't actually a member of the tribe. I thus had one more chance: was anyone in his family by chance Jewish?

Jackpot! His wife was Jewish, and he had three Jewish children. He himself was Russian Orthodox Christian, but he knew that his children were Jewish. The wife didn't go to church with him, and neither did the kids. She was nonpracticing, though: no Shabbat candles, no Passover seder, no matzah, no Yom Kippur, no temple attendance, no nothin'.

I started explaining The Chai Center menu to him, and he began to wax more enthusiastic. By the end of the ride, he was absolutely into the prospect of coming to Shabbat dinner with his Jewish wife and Jewish kids.

The opportunity to educate Jewish kids who might have grown up barely knowing they were Jews is priceless; it's called saving the lives of three Jewish children!

I love when that happens!

CHAPTER 35

"TAKE ME TO THE JEWS!" TAOS, NEW MEXICO

In 1993, I was invited to speak at a *shabbaton* in Santa Fe, New Mexico. I was very excited because I always wanted to go to Taos—people told me it was an energy vortex. That I had to see . . .

We had a friend, Chaya, whom my son had made a *shidduch* for, and she had a bed-and-breakfast in Taos that she essentially wasn't using because she was living in Jerusalem. Chaya had a manager looking after the place and welcomed me to stay there after the retreat. I never charged for speaking anywhere (my way of giving charity), but I asked for a rental car so I could get to Santa Fe and then Taos, both hours away from the airport. When I got to the car rental, I was told the car I had requested wasn't available, but I could have an upgrade to a car with four-wheel drive if I wanted. Sure, why not? I didn't know that would be important later.

The *shabbaton* weekend was quite impressive. The organizers had koshered an Italian restaurant and had eighty-three people, a nice crowd in a place with not so many Jews. On Sunday, I left for a few days in Taos to see it and perhaps pick up some extra energy.

When I got to Taos, I asked people where I could see the best sunset, because I *love* sunsets. They told me to go to the Rio Grande Gorge Bridge, an arch bridge about ten miles out of town. No one was on the road, so I put the car on cruise control at one hundred miles per hour; thank G-d, no speed traps. When I got to the bridge, I saw that the sunset was over the next ridge, and to get there, I'd have to go off road and through the sagebrush. But I could do that! I had a car with four-wheel drive!

I was driving to the ridge where I could see the sun before it set, and in the distance, I saw a man with his thumb out. At first, I thought it was a mirage, but then I saw that no, someone was really there, a man in his sixties, strange looking, with his thumb out.

I thought to myself, *Should I stop?* He looks kind of wild, but if I don't stop, I'll never know why he's here. As I grew closer, I looked him over. Well, I thought, if he starts up with me, I think I can overpower him. So I stopped the car.

The man got in, took one look at me, and said, "Cool, man—I used to be a Jew."

He told me his story as we drove across the sagebrush. He wasn't an MOT (Member of the Tribe), but he used to live in Berkeley, California, and studied with Rabbi Citron at the Chabad House there for six years. (As it happens, I helped found that Chabad House.) He told me that he had decided not to convert, but Rabbi Citron had given him a G-d he could believe in.

He also said he was a sort of unofficial "rabbi" for the Jews who lived in earth homes in the area. A bunch of people formed an alternative community in the fields of sagebrush, living in homes that were partially built into the earth, and the community contained at least fifty Jews. These were folks who were very anti-government, fighting to legalize drugs, and so on. I couldn't believe it! "Take me to the Jews," I told him.

I spent the whole night, until dawn, going with this guy from home to home, meeting the Jews: a woman from Russia, nine months pregnant; a scientist in a wheelchair; on and on, one unique individual after another, all Jewish. I taught them how to make blessings over the herbs they grew. I had a great time.

Sure enough, my new friend was their rabbi. He encouraged them on holidays and Shabbat to do Jewish things. Weeks later, we mailed him hand-baked *shmura* matzah (not the factory-made stuff) to give out to his congregants.

The next year, Olivia and I were invited to Taos to lead a *shabbaton* weekend. We stayed at the famous Sagebrush Inn, and as we pulled into the parking lot, who should be there but my friend, the non-Jewish rabbi. He had no idea that a Jewish *shabbaton* was about to happen there. I don't know whether Taos is an energy vortex, but G-d's energy was certainly at work.

I love when that happens!

ISRAEL AND THE FOUR HOLY CITIES

CHAPTER 36

THE POWER OF THE WALL: MY LAST DAY THERE

Olivia recalls:

> *When we were first asked to teach at Ascent in Safed, Shlomo said, "No, we can't possibly go; I can't take off work," and I said, "Yeah, we'll go; we'll go for two weeks." OK, he agreed to go, so we went for two weeks.*
>
> *Then he loved it, his teaching was just extraordinary, and the next summer he said, "OK, I'll go for two weeks." Then the next summer, I made the trip for like three or four weeks. By the next summer, I realized he only asked me what day we were going and what day we'd be returning. He actually had no idea that little by little I just extended it to nearly three months. And that's how we ended up going for so long. I just realized, even though he kept saying, "I can't miss work; I have to be here," he just had no idea how long we were away.*

There's a certain strange sense of power, when you are suddenly alone, and it comes to you—you realize that you know a personal fact about people who are complete strangers to you, whom you don't know. A fact they themselves do not know.

OK, let's be more specific. Let's begin:

Of the millions of Jews who presently reside in the United States, (not counting Birthright groups), 90 percent of them have never been to Israel. Of that 90 percent, 80 percent have no intention of ever going to Israel (at least until they first visit Las Vegas, Maui, the Greek islands, and all the other places on their lists).

After the miracle of the Six-Day War, American Jews began to visit Israel in greater numbers. I don't really keep track, but I have probably been to our homeland thirty times. One of the mandatory sightseeing stops is the Western Wall, the *Kotel*, on the Temple Mount.

Because I really enjoy validating our tradition's dictum that "there is no Torah study like that studied in Israel," it is always difficult to leave Israel and return to America. To solidify the soul energization I get in Israel and to give it a *zetz* of (spiritual) Viagra-like staying power, I've formulated a personal *minhag* (custom): the day I leave, I go hang out at the Western Wall. I give myself about three hours. During that time, I don't socialize; I pray and meditate. I need that cementing and defense-building time for myself.

Other times when I go to the Kotel, I spend some time with the American Jewish tourists, especially the ones who look kind of lost there, as if they are clueless and sincerely want to know what they should be doing while there.

You hear them say the same thing, one tourist after another. When you hear the exact same quote from an array of people over decades, it becomes a cliché. Are you ready for the most verbalized sentiment in reaction to the experience of being at the Western Wall (many saying it with tears in their eyes)?

"I'm not a religious person, so I never imagined that I would be so *moved!*"

And they still have no clue what moved them so much, many not having been to synagogue in years.

This fact about our people, across the board, whatever their level of Jewish practice or non-practice, reveals something about the much-talked-about, fascinating, and indestructible Jewish soul.

It's actually not that relevant if, in your family, the religion has not been observed for a couple of generations. There is a quintessential point in the deepest depths of your soul that is always connected. However, it rarely comes out. That's why I call Yom Kippur the "annual coming-out party for closet Jewry." Yom Kippur is a time when your *pinteleh yid*, your

Jewish spark, gets tickled and aroused, and you can sometimes experience a presence you're not usually aware of.

The job requirements for visiting Israel should read, "No experience necessary." You don't have to read Hebrew or understand Yiddish. You don't even have to like falafel or camel rides or hummus.

My standard query to the American Jewish tourists is: "Why are you crying when you come back from the Wall?" I always get the same three-word answer, delivered with the same quizzical expression: "I don't know!" Then they want me to tell them why they were sobbing uncontrollably.

Here's an example; wouldn't you know it happened on my last day in Israel one summer:

I was doing my thing at the Wall, and out of the corner of my eye, I caught a glimpse of a man in his early fifties walking around, and I instantly *knew* that I could help him. But I knew it would take precious time—and I was leaving soon. So I put my nose back into a holy book and tried to meditate about how I could take the G-dliness of Israel with me back to Los Angeles.

Suddenly, I felt someone tapping me on my shoulder. I turned around, and it was the guy in his fifties. I then smiled because, at the Wall, you can run, but you can't hide. At the zenith of G-d's presence on planet Earth, you are going to do what *He* wants you to do.

When I first saw this guy, I picked up that he must be a nonreligious tourist from New York.

Then I saw that every once in a while, he looked up at the plaza in the back, above the Wall, and started to gesture furiously at what appeared to be his wife. She seemed angry and impatient and wanting to go, pointing to her watch and waving him toward her. I figured she came and saw the Wall—and after five minutes, she was done and wanted to go back to the Sheraton to shop and sit at the pool and chill.

He, on the other hand, had been bitten by the BUG!

The first thing he said to me was, "Do you speak English?" with a Brooklyn accent. I realized that I was stuck.

He said he was in his early fifties, and it was his first trip to Israel, and he didn't really know why he came. But he actually did come looking for *something* (although he didn't tell his wife that he was "looking for something," because she just wasn't that type).

They got to Israel ten days before and immediately went to Club Med in Eilat. The "something" he was (secretly) looking for—"IT"—wasn't there.

Then they went to the Hilton in Tel Aviv for a few days. IT wasn't there either.

They were supposed to be at the Wall for fifteen minutes. Now his wife was impatient with him because she wanted to go already, and he'd been at the Kotel for more than an hour.

But he finally found the reason that he had come to Israel.

He said to me emotionally, "IT is here!"

Then he said, "Now that I've *found* IT, I need you to explain to me what IT *is*!"

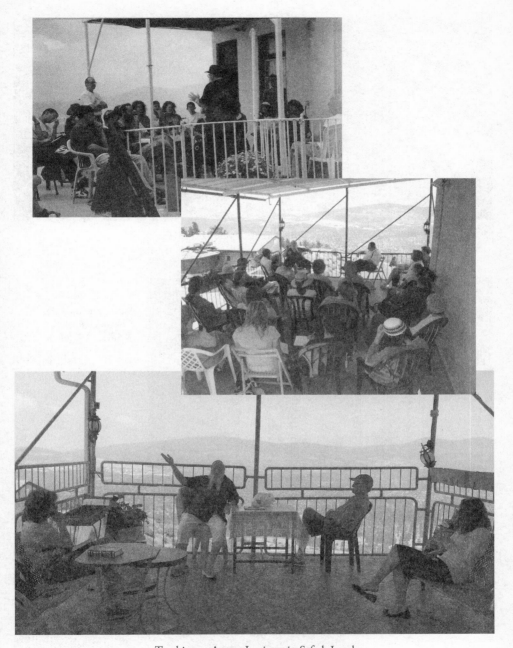

Teaching at Ascent Institute in Safed, Israel

Schwartzie in Ascent's rooftop classroom

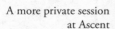

Ascent renamed the
rooftop classroom
"Schwartzie's Porch"

A more private session
at Ascent

Some private study time in the Ascent library

Hanging with the locals in Safed

With soul brother Asi

Love my hat!

Havdalah in Safed

I wrapped this man during the Lebanon War.

Now that's what I call breakfast!

The view from Safed

Praying at the tomb
of Maimonides in
Tiberias

Almost ready for bar mitzvah service at the Western Wall

Shopping at the
Machane Yehuda
Shuk In Jerusalem

With Weinberg family at Western Wall

With Weinberg family in Hebron

Dancing with the locals

Olivia with some new IDF friends

Enjoying a latte with
my buddy in Jerusalem

Writing a personal note to the Holy Arizal, founder of
Lurianic Kabbala, buried in Safed, Israel

CHAPTER 37

JERUSALEM MAGIC

One weekend, we were in the holy city of Jerusalem for Shabbat. It just doesn't lose its powerful magic! People who know a little about Shabbat could have a nice experience even in Los Angeles (especially at our Shabbat table). But nothing compares to being in Israel on the holy Shabbat. Now imagine not just being in the Holy Land on Shabbat but being in Jerusalem on Shabbat! That is a powerful experience, even for Jews who are clueless about what Shabbat is.

Saturday night, we went to the Old City of Jerusalem to visit very good friends. They met on a beach in Puerto Rico when they were nineteen and twenty years old. When they played Jewish Geography, they discovered they were both Jews from Detroit. Mazel tov, they got married; he became a podiatrist and then a foot surgeon.

They had four kids, moved to Laguna Beach, California, and *then* started worrying about whom these beautiful, innocent, sweet Jewish children would marry. Meanwhile, he became very successful, and they bought a beautiful home near the beach and were having a very nice, blessed life zipping around town in a very cool white Porsche. They started getting more interested in their Judaism. But Laguna isn't exactly the heart of Jewish America, nearly the opposite.

After a while, they decided to give the kids a heavy dose of Jewishness and travel to Israel for a visit. They arrived in the Jewish homeland, and that's when things changed. She said, "I'm not leaving! You go back to

Laguna: sell the house, the business, and the Porsche; we're staying here."
That was thirty years ago.

Surprise! Every one of their children married someone Jewish.

They live in a really beautiful, spacious home in the Old City of
Jerusalem. Israel had foot doctors, but it didn't really have a specialist
devoted to foot surgery. Although his Hebrew wasn't great, he went on
Israeli TV and developed cash customers from all over the Middle East.
Baruch haShem, after a while he was, once again, doing extremely well.

Last Saturday, when we visited, we all traipsed up to his rooftop. The
view is of the Western Wall and the Temple Mount. It is truly breathtaking and inspiring. It's like living in classical history. We were all there just
chilling and enjoying.

Suddenly, we all saw a comet in the night sky over Jerusalem. It was
riveting to see a large light with a long tail streak across the heavens and
slowly break up. It was my first comet.

*Baruch atah, Adonai Elokeinu, Melech ha-olam, shehecheyanu v'kiymanu
v'higiyanu lazman hazeh:* Praised are You, Lord our G-d, Ruler of the
Universe, who gives us life, sustains us, and brings us to this time.

* * *

About thirty years ago, there was a Jewish couple who lived in Venice
Beach. She was Israeli and he was American. We met them at a party in Los
Angeles.

They had a seven-year-old son who suddenly became ill. The mom
called me to put up a *mezuzah* on his bedroom door. (No atheists in
foxholes, right?) Shortly afterward, they got divorced. She moved back to
Israel with the son, and they had no contact for seven years.

Unbeknownst to them both, they had each started following an
Indian guru. Then she moved back to Los Angeles, and by "accident" (HA!)
they met . . . started hanging out . . . and *remarried.* The guru died, and
they started getting back into some Jewish stuff; that's when we met them
again. They kept progressing in their Jewish consciousness and practice
until she convinced him to move back to Israel with her. Now the boy was
a strapping young fellow of nineteen and a great athlete who became a star
baseball player and traveled to Europe with the Israeli team to compete.

During the second intifada, the son was walking along the pedestrian
mall in Jerusalem, Ben Yehuda Street, when a suicide bomber blew himself
up in the crowded street near him. Although injured, the young man ran
through the dead bodies and moaning wounded to escape and to get help,

only to be caught by another suicide bomber who detonated himself three minutes later.

He survived but had to endure many surgeries during the next year. When it was all over, the surgeons presented him with a bag containing the shrapnel, nails, screws, and ball bearings that they had removed from his body. It actually weighed almost *half a kilogram*. Miraculously, he was physically OK and could walk, see, hear, and function, but his baseball career was over.

The young man married an American woman whose parents had made aliyah to Israel when she was five. But no one (including all his doctors) really knew whether he would ever be able to have children.

I hadn't seen this family for a number of years, and one day this past summer when we were in "exile" in Jerusalem as refugees from the war with Lebanon, I went to the Kotel to pray, and by "accident" (HA!), right there was the *entire family* at the naming of the healthy *baby girl* born to our former baseball player. Mazel tov!

CHAPTER 38

SAFED: HOLY CITY OF THE SPIRIT

I revered Jerusalem, but I loved the northern town of Safed with the soul of an ardent lover.

Everyone knows that Jerusalem is a holy city. Actually, all the Western religions recognize Jerusalem as a holy city. But most people don't know that the Holy Land (no, I'm not talking about Brooklyn) has four holy cities: Jerusalem, Hebron, Tiberias, and Safed.

Kabbalah, in the *Zohar*, its foundational text along with the Bible, tells us that the universe is composed of four elements: fire, water, earth, and air. Beginning in the sixteenth century, Jewish mystics began to associate the four elements with other things that came in fours, such as compass directions, phases of the moon, and seasons of the year. (The *Zohar* had already related them to the four ministering angels, Uriel, Raphael, Gabriel, and Michael, and to the four corners of the earth, as mentioned in the Hebrew Bible.)

When the "holy cities" idea came up in the 1600s, each holy city became associated with one of the four elements. Thus, Jerusalem, where Temple sacrifices occurred, equals fire; Hebron, where the patriarchs and matriarchs are buried, is earth; Tiberias, on the Sea of Galilee, is about water; and Safed, up in the mountains, equals air. Think about it: air—wind—spirit—spirituality!

Safed is where the most famous kabbalists, the followers of Rabbi Isaac Luria, settled, prayed, and studied in the 1500s. Today it's still a center for Jewish spirituality, and I was able to spend more than twenty summers there as scholar-in-residence at the Ascent Institute, a study center for people ages eighteen to twenty-eight.

Safed is really a small town: no movie theaters, no traffic lights, and no car rentals, with a population (including in the surrounding hills) of perhaps thirty thousand. It has the second-highest elevation in Israel, with breathtaking views in every direction. Around sundown especially, it's exquisitely beautiful.

The old city of Safed is four centuries old, with streets no bigger than alleys, paved completely with cobblestones. The old city houses an artists' colony with homes, studios, and galleries. One main street, called Jerusalem Street, circles the whole town. It's so small that it takes only twenty-five minutes to walk the entire street, which is lined with restaurants, cafés, shops, and souvenir stands.

One of my favorite places was a small café with a wood bar made from the trunk of a single huge tree, polished and shellacked so the pretty grain shows through. The view from the high ceiling down to your waist isn't through a picture window, but simply open air. There's nothing between you and the twin peaks of Mount Miron, the burial site of the holy Rashbi, Rabbi Simeon ben Yochai, who is credited with writing the *Zohar*.

Then there's the new city, with high-rises, supermarkets, and gas stations—and also one decent hotel called the Rimon Inn that was recently bought by Howard Johnson and upgraded to three-and-a-half stars (but charges five-star prices). The good news is that there are dozens of bed-and-breakfast rooms for rent, again with very friendly Jews who keep feeding you amazing, glorious, homemade breakfasts as if you were a long-lost cousin.

As I mentioned, Safed is the birthplace and headquarters of modern Kabbalah. The mystics of the day all knew each other; they studied and prayed together in the sixteenth century. Today we know most of the details of their lives: who their parents, wives, children, and teachers were. Virtually all of them were published, and their books are still the basic texts of pure, authentic Kabbalah, universally accepted. It is thrilling to know that these historic kabbalists walked the same streets four-hundred-plus years ago that I have walked and prayed in synagogues named after them that are still in operation, where I have prayed three times a day.

And they are buried in the ancient cemetery on the edge of the city, their graves considered holy places, visited by thousands. The kabbalists say that if you pray for someone at the grave of one of the mystic saints of Safed on his yahrzeit, the mystic in that grave will intercede and grant blessings on that someone's behalf.

That sense of mystical power is probably why Safed is so moving, even for Jews with little or no Jewish background. They start to remember and compare the "unusual" experiences they've had thus far, and in Safed, those weird thoughts and visions and coincidences take on a spiritual/religious/ mystical/kabbalistic nature that they weren't familiar with previously. It is quite fascinating to see people change some of their ideas, even their ways of thinking, in a few days, in the vortex of energy, the spiritual force-field that is the beautiful mountaintop holy city of Safed.

In addition to the great spiritual fruits to be had there, the success in plain old simple outreach is mind-blowing, and it's with hardly any effort—kind of like "shooting fish in a barrel."

What would take me two years in Los Angeles in terms of moving a person forward in Judaism takes place nearly instantly—in five days. In the holy city, the product sells itself. People take the plunge even if they're not ready. Almost everyone who comes to Safed for one day, or a few days, extends his or her stay in this mystical city. It's almost as if it's impossible to leave.

Every summer, on the plane to Israel for my annual weeks in Safed, I would feel like a long-married spouse who was about to be reunited with his beloved after a forced separation. Couples separated by war, business, emigration, and sheer circumstance—were their joy and levels of excitement, their wanting to be close again, greater than mine on returning to Safed? Its balance of peace and spiritual energy was unparalleled anywhere else on earth.

Unless Hezbollah started sending missiles from southern Lebanon . . .

CHAPTER 39

MY SUMMER VACATION
AND THE LEBANON WAR

On July 12, 2006, the terrorist organization Hezbollah attacked Israeli tanks and villages along the Israel-Lebanon border, killing three IDF soldiers, while two others were taken hostage. Another five Israeli soldiers died in a rescue attempt. Hezbollah demanded a prisoner exchange, the release of all Lebanese held by Israel for the return of the two abducted IDF soldiers, but Israel refused. It responded with attacks on Hezbollah military targets and Lebanese civilian infrastructure, along with a ground invasion of southern Lebanon and a naval and air blockade. Hezbollah continued to send missiles into northern Israel and to engage the IDF in guerrilla warfare until the United Nations negotiated a ceasefire on August 14. The conflict caused the deaths of 165 Israelis, including 44 civilians, with another 1,500 Israelis injured. Between 300,000 and 500,000 Israelis were displaced from their homes in northern Israel.

Olivia and I were in Safed, eight miles from the Lebanese border, for our yearly Ascent Institute residency when the rockets started flying.

Safed is known as a summer resort because, as it's on a mountain, the weather is much cooler in the summer than it is in Tel Aviv or almost anywhere else in the country. At this point, it was a ghost town, with more than 90 percent of the residents having fled to save their lives. Among Safed's sixty synagogues (many of them in continual use for the last four centuries and more), a bare-bones minyan was meeting in the three that were not closed and locked up.

A Chasidic village of about one thousand families near Tel Aviv had taken in seven hundred households from Safed. Almost every family in the village had strangers staying in their small apartments. There was also a huge tent city on the beach near Tel Aviv that baked mercilessly during the daytime sun, with adults and many children lying about with nothing to do.

When we left Safed after two days of the attacks, we took very few of our belongings. We "knew" that this type of insanity couldn't last but a day or two before it would be stopped, and then we'd return.

We never dreamed that this would become a *war*, with large missile projectiles filled with sixty pounds of explosives and thousands of ball bearings being fired indiscriminately at civilian cities, including Israel's third largest city, Haifa. Cities in the north of Israel that I've heard of but have never been to were now front-page news and becoming familiar names.

But the personal stories of these people are the most profoundly moving and give what was occurring the correct perspective of reality.

In Jerusalem, I met the exiled refugees of the cities Kiryat Shmona, Nahariya, Tiberias, Carmiel, Rosh Pina, and others in northern Israel. All these cities are not small by Israeli standards, with populations between ten thousand and thirty thousand. Each one of them had been mercilessly pounded for almost four weeks. The residents slept in cramped, airless, hot, muggy bomb shelters. Many of the people either knew the victims who'd been killed or at least one of the wounded.

At this point, all these lovely communities were ugly, eerily quiet ghost towns. Hundreds of thousands of people were displaced and homeless. In a small country of six million, it was a national disaster.

* * *

I had a great class of about thirty interested, bright American Jews, studying Kabbalah up on a porch with an amazing view of Mount Miron, a four-hour hike away. For a number of hours, we had heard explosions in the distance; I convinced my class that it was the IDF bombing Hezbollah in southern Lebanon.

Then the first Katyusha rocket hit Safed.

This adorable, quaint vortex of divine energy had not experienced anything akin to this since 1948, during the War of Israeli Independence.

The third rocket hit about two blocks away, and everyone freaked and ran to the basement of the building, some crying, some screaming. There we regrouped, but it was plain to see that some people's lives were instantly changed forever.

If you are close enough to hear the whistle of a flying Katyusha, that means you are too close. And seconds later, when it hits and you are still alive, having escaped the tremendous shrapnel that it sprays in order to kill and maim, the terrifying noise of the explosion will stay with you the rest of your life. (Of course, that condition has a name now: post-traumatic stress disorder.)

The next Shabbat, I wanted to go back to Safed, although Hezbollah was still shelling the city, and Olivia said, "I *never* want to hear that noise again."

The next day, basically everyone left Safed.

Flash forward to one day before the ceasefire (my luck).

There are different types of charity. There is charity with your money, and then there is charity carried out with your body.

I was in a cab a few days before the ceasefire, and the radio was turned up loud. It took me a while to figure out what was going on, but then I got it. The radio announcer was just reading a list of names, ranks, and ages of fallen Israeli soldiers.

As I sat in the back listening (especially to the ages; they were mostly young, twenty-somethings), I felt helpless, and I noticed that the cab driver was crying. It must've been contagious because I started crying quietly to myself about the wives who would never marry them and their beautiful children who would never be born.

I figured that because I didn't really have a lot of greenbacks, but I was in the country already, the least I could do to help out is visit the soldiers right before they went into battle, cheer them up, put tefillin on them, and so on. I wasn't prepared for how sincerely appreciative they all would be. I was also not prepared to be in an active war zone. But more about that later.

My longtime friend, Meir Rhodes, and I drove up toward the north in a civilian car. We heard that because there was talk of a ceasefire, the shelling on the cities in the north was particularly intense—though we really had no way of perceiving what that meant in real terms. We three were Americans, and none of us had ever been in any army, let alone in active combat. We decided that we needed a little extra juice (a.k.a. Mitzvah Merit for protection).

Because we had to pass through the city of Tiberias on our way north, we stopped at the tomb of Rabbi Meir, the master of miracles, to pray. Tiberias is on the shore of the Sea of Galilee, also known as Lake Kinneret.

It's also an extremely crowded summer resort with many luxurious, five-star-plus, high-rise hotels. The population is more than 100,000. But with 70 percent of the population having fled, Tiberias, like Safed, was an eerie ghost town. All the traffic lights were just blinking yellow. I guess the city officials figured that as virtually all the civilian cars were off the streets, lights were no longer needed. As we drove along the lake, we were surprised to see that the usually crowded beach was completely empty.

Usually, right outside the entrance to Rabbi Meir's tomb, there are several tourist-trap stalls selling kipot, mezuzahs, and incense. Everything was closed. But inside there were eight men who were waiting for two more so they could have a service with a proper minyan of ten.

Just then, I met a new guy who popped in, whom I knew from Safed. So my two friends went into the little synagogue next to Rabbi Meir's tomb and made the minyan, and I stepped out with my buddy from Safed to talk.

I asked him the obvious question with the two-letter non-word that is so explicit and descriptive in Yiddish: "Nu?" Translation: So how's it living in Safed these days? He said that on the second day of the war, a missile hit three houses away from his three-story, a beautiful house with an amazing view. His two kids were terrified and his wife totally freaked, so they left a few hours later.

Right after the blast, he went outside to see what happened and saw four young children, ages four through eleven, covered in dust and soot but standing—standing still, actually, unmoving, expressionless, as if frozen in shock. Then he saw that underneath the gray dust there was red slowly seeping through, so he took all of them to the only hospital in the (formerly) quaint little town that is Safed. He was very thankful to G-d that it wasn't a direct hit through his own home—had it been, he wouldn't have been able to tell me the story.

After praying at the tomb of Rabbi Meir, we drove for another forty-five minutes due north to the border of Israel and Lebanon. Now there were no civilian cars, only army vehicles and tanks and foot soldiers, and they all stared in wonder at us civilians in our "regular" car. The noise of battle was deafening. It was mostly our cannons firing, but somehow it was still quite terrifying.

We first passed the city of Kiryat Shmona. It used to be a very nice city, with about fifty thousand inhabitants. It was one of the hardest hit by the Hezbollah shelling for an entire month and was even more deserted than Tiberias or Safed was. We didn't see one civilian in the streets, but we did see what happens when a detached single-family home takes a direct hit from a Katyusha rocket. It was a pathetic skeleton that spoke silently of violence, intrusion, and death.

A few minutes past Kiryat Shmona was a little town called Metulah. It's the farthest town north before the border, and the army had taken over the empty town. We drove for another few minutes, and suddenly, on the side of the road to our right, there was an enormous, wide-open field that was serving as the staging ground. We parked on the side of the empty road and entered the camp. We had thought the noise couldn't get any louder, but here there was a significant elevation in decibels.

The staging ground had many huge tents, with about fifty soldiers in each tent, plus one hundred tanks. When night fell, the troops would jog all night, with heavy backpacks on, into Lebanon to the battlefield, into active combat.

The mood in the tents was somber: young men, mostly ages eighteen to twenty-three, contemplating their last few hours before the inevitable unknown. Would they come back alive? Would they come back wounded, maimed for life, without limbs?

I had been a rabbi and public speaker for the past forty-six years of my life, and this had to be one of my toughest gigs by far.

The three of us walked into the first tent with our tefillin. The first response of these battle-hardened soldiers was incredulity. Their faces held a unanimous, unspoken question: "What in G-d's name are you guys doing here?"

I saw immediately that we had the edge, because even those who were not connected to religion had figured out what a few older men with beards and kipot and carrying tefillin were doing there. These soldiers recognized and very much appreciated people coming to visit them and to help them pray for their safe return just before they went into a fierce battle.

My Hebrew isn't that good, and I knew that about 70 to 80 percent of the fellows understood English, so instead of pussy-footing around, I announced loudly, "We Americans only have the Fourth of July once a year, but you guys have it every day here! It's *very loud!*" A few officers smiled at the naïve, dumb, religious Americans, which broke the ice, and the soldiers began to feel sorry for us crazy, fanatic, but well-meaning civilians who cared enough about them to make this field trip.

After a few seconds, some of the friendlier men said, "We don't even hear it anymore." Now that is quite hard to believe. Others said that when the Hezbollah get really close, now that is called LOUD! At this point, I couldn't imagine what they were talking about.

Then a very tough officer with a commanding personality and a mucho-macho bald head stood up. He was about six-foot-two, built like a brick s--thouse, and all could see he was not into anything light or easy. He said, "I'm not religious, and I don't put on tefillin, but out of respect for you that you came here, I'll do it."

Of course, after him, everyone else slowly came forward to ask us to help put on the tefillin, as only two of them knew how to do it. It was quite moving for the three of us Americans. You could actually see trepidation in the eyes of the young soldiers. This was no fun-and-games scene.

Some soldiers whispered to us that we really should leave soon because there was intelligence that the enemy knew about this staging area and were going to try to knock it out soon, and it was going to get dangerous. I couldn't understand what could get more dangerous than being there just then was.

We found out pretty quickly.

The Israeli cannons started pumping away without a stop, really pounding the enemy positions that were only about ten miles away. The noise became almost unbearable. I asked a soldier what the change was about.

He said that the enemy was trying to hit this staging area, and to stop its forces, our cannons were trying to keep them busy. The IDF did a great job, but two missiles did get through and landed about the equivalent of two blocks away, starting a fire in the open field.

We had been there three hours and had been to most of the tents already. But the bombs that fell close by definitely influenced my decision to persuade my friends to call it a day, get back to the car, and try to outrun the bombs. We hugged some of the fellows and wished them well.

As we passed through Metulah, we heard air raid sirens, and we heard them again as we went through Kiryat Shmona. But instead of stopping to find an air raid shelter, we just drove faster, and thank G-d, it was bashert that we were not reduced to body parts, and I got to share this story.

CHAPTER 40

HEBRON: STAIRS OF HOPE

In 1993, Olivia and I brought our son Yosef, age 12, to Israel.

Yosef and I spent Shabbat in the Jewish community of Hebron, now an almost all-Arab city surrounding a small enclave of 70 Jewish families. A man named David Shirelle picked us up in Kiryat Arba, a safer adjoining Jewish settlement where we had been staying to bring us to Hebron just a few minutes away.

On the way to Hebron, we discovered that we both grew up in Atlantic City, and my family bought their kosher meat from David's grandparents, and that my father had officiated at David's parents' wedding.

David and I became close friends, and the 1993 trip was the first of many visits I made to Hebron, one of Israel's historic holy cities and site of the Cave of Machpelah, where the Biblical ancestors of Jews are buried.

David Shirelle tells a story known to only a few people.

> I think everyone knew Shlomo's favorite time of the year was summertime, the months spent in Israel. Although the majority of his time was spent teaching in Safed, every summer he would take off two weeks to breathe the air of Hebron, learning, praying, talking to everyone. He was at home.
>
> His daily schedule would include a dunk in the mikvah in the Abraham Avinu neighborhood; praying in the Machpelah, the burial place of Abraham, Isaac,

*Jacob, Rebekah, Leah, and Sarah;
learning Torah in the Menucha
Rochel shul; reciting some psalms at
the grave of Jesse and Ruth; eating
at the Shirelle home; and, of course,
talking to every soldier along the
way. I was always amazed that
within hours of arriving, he knew
every soldier's name and where each
one came from.*

*One summer afternoon,
toward the end of a week in
Hebron, Shlomo walked in my
house after returning from the grave
of Ruth and Jesse in the Admot
Yishai neighborhood, Tel Rumeida,
which happens to be the first palace
of King David; it was there in
Hebron for many years before it was
in Jerusalem.*

*And Shlomo said to me,
"What a long walk up! Isn't there
a shortcut?" I explained to him
that there actually is, by taking the
steps right outside my house in the
Beit Hadassah neighborhood. It is
half the distance, but there is one
problem: years ago, when the Arabs
saw that the Jews were enjoying the
shortcut, they built a wall blocking
the way. "Young teenagers are still
able to climb over, but for you and
me, Shlomo, as young as we like to
feel, forget it; it's not for us," I said.*

*Now, the Jews in Hebron are
known to be tough, but here we had
a problem. The courts had decided*

*that the wall was now built, and
the soldiers had been given clear
orders to protect it and even arrest
anyone who tried to damage it
or take it down. The local Jewish
residents tried everything: speaking
to the top generals in the Army,
Knesset members, ministers, and
so on. But it seemed that the wall
was there to stay. After hearing these
details, Shlomo said, "It can't be. It
doesn't make sense. I'll have to check
it out myself." And then he was out
the door.*

*A few minutes went by, and
Shlomo was back in my house, very
upset. "You're right; I tried walking
up the steps," he said. "What a
great shortcut, but halfway up,
there's a wall blocking the path. I
can't get over the wall. We need to
do something."*

*I said, "Good luck, Shlomo;
we've been trying for years to solve
the problem. Don't waste your
time." I told him that so many
people had walked up these steps
to find themselves blocked, causing
them to turn around and come all
the way down again, that the steps
actually had been given a name:
"The Steps of Despair."*

*An hour went by, and Shlomo
was back in my home again, this
time full of dust and dirt. "Shlomo,
what happened?" I asked.*

"Baruch haShem, we took the wall down. The shortcut is now open to all!"

"Shlomo, what are you talking about?"

Very excited, he explained to me that he had spoken to the soldiers, and they knocked the wall down. "You're telling me that you simply spoke to the soldiers and they said, 'No problem,' and they knocked the wall down?"

"Yes, that's what happened." Shlomo went on to explain, "I spoke to Mutti, and he gave the orders to knock it down."

"I can't believe this! Who's Mutti?"

"Mutti is the head officer," Shlomo explained. Shlomo, of course, knew every one of them by name. He continued, "Well, I was sitting and talking to the soldiers, a great bunch of guys: Shimon, Rulet, Heshy, Sholom—did you know Sholom is a Jersey boy? Anyway, they saw how the wall really bothered me, so they spoke to Mutti, their officer. Mutti arrived at the scene and spoke on the Army radio to Itzik. Itzik called Avi, who phoned Dudu and told him to bring a big, five-kilo hammer. Next thing you know, no wall."

Shlomo was so happy, but I continued not to believe, telling him he was dreaming. "Let's go look together; I have to see this for myself." As I went up the steps with Shlomo, I couldn't believe my eyes. Sure enough, no wall.

After asking the soldiers what happened, they answered, "Shlomo asked us to knock it down, so we did."

"What?" I said, facing the soldiers. "This guy has been here a week, and you do whatever he wants?"

"Well, he's such a nice guy," the soldiers said.

"I'm also a nice guy," I answered. "I've been asking you to knock down the wall for the last ten years, with no success."

Finally, one of the soldiers explained, "Shlomo may have only been here for a week, but every day this week, he bought lunch for the entire unit. One day pizza, next day falafel, and then malawach (Yemeni fried flatbread) together with ice cream and soda. He showed his true and sincere love to us."

I looked at Shlomo in amazement. "Shlomo, is that true? Every day, you have been buying lunch for the entire unit?"

With his modest smile and special laugh, he answered, "Hey, look what you can do with fifty dollars in Hebron."

From that day on, the name of the steps changed. Anyone visiting

Hebron can pass by the steps and see the new name embedded in the wall: *The Steps of Hope*. Madrigot ha-tikvah *is what those steps are named now.*

That was Shlomo. Whether in his home Friday night with all the guests, on the beach, or in the casbah of Hebron, he taught us all what true love, ahavat Yisrael, *is all about. Not just talking about love, or learning about it in a book, but getting out there, finding Jews in need, loving and caring for them, and showing them the steps of hope in life. He taught us all that true love can knock down even the biggest walls.*

The Stairs of Hope in Hebron

FASCINATING VIGNETTES

CHAPTER 41

WOODSTOCK 1969

Avraham Rosenblum, who appeared at Woodstock II in 1994, was introduced to Schwartzie while the Diaspora Yeshiva Band was on its first US tour in late 1979. "It was great to be a young Jewish man leading a ba'al teshuvah rock band on the road with a Gibson electric guitar and a microphone," Avraham said.

The band would exhort its listeners to "get high with a little help from G-d!"

Olivia Schwartz, a friend of Avraham, made the introduction when the band arrived in Los Angeles, but later Avraham realized that he knew Rabbi Schwartz from somewhere . . . somewhere in Sullivan County, New York, from about ten years earlier.

Avraham wrote about his 1969 Woodstock experience, starting with his arrival at the festival, which he attended on a whim while driving to Canada.

As I waded into the growing sea of happy people who dressed and talked a lot like me, I had an epiphany that this was going to be a life-changing event. I was elated to be part of this new social order. I belonged in it. I had worked hard to forget my origins as a [second]-generation, Yiddish-speaking, Holocaust survivors' kid from Northeast Philadelphia. My music and this culture were my way out and into the melting pot of America. My bandmates and friends were mostly children or grandchildren of Italian, Irish, and Scottish immigrants. Few were Jews. We were all looking for the same thing. And, me being me, I interpreted my Woodstock experience as spiritual, in the sense that our generation was in search of peace, love, and harmony.

One thing led to another quickly: the crowd got larger; the music more intense; the weather rainier; and my sense of direction, which normally was quite acute, became limited to "up or down" mode. On Saturday night, after some hours of searching, I found my car. Six very helpful hippies helped me roll it out of the mud. I clearly remember feeling grateful to "someone" that my guitars and belongings were still there. I was wet, chilled, and hungry, and stupidly determined to continue northward to Quebec, even though the hour was getting late. But a few miles up the road, I realized that the snaking center line was not a good sign, as my head began to hurt and I started to feel feverish. I turned around and somehow found Monticello General Hospital where, after a cursory look by a staffer, I was very kindly shown to a chair in the waiting room, in which I fell asleep.

I awoke as people began to enter the room at 9 a.m. I noticed a number of them were religious. And there I was, with my unwashed shoulder-length hair, love beads, well-worn denims, and muddy shoes, when I caught the glance of a young yeshiva student, whom I instantly greeted: "Shalom! Vos machts du?" (Peace! How are you?)

"Vos tust'de doh?" (What are you doing here?) he asked with surprise.

"Ich hob kekumen tzu Woodstock!" (I attended Woodstock!) I answered forthrightly, as if to impress him.

"Un vus host'du gezucht bei Woodstock?" (And what were you looking for at Woodstock?) he asked with genuine interest.

Switching to English, I said something about finding G-d in the big experience of unity and not being limited to a synagogue. Unfazed, but needing to fulfill his mission of visiting a sick friend, the yeshiva boy apologized for not having the time to continue our conversation and wrote down a phone number and address on a piece of notepaper that he handed to me while recommending, "If you're really looking for G-d and spirituality, check this out. Shalom. Zei gezundt!" (Be well!)

That was before a trip to Israel changed the life of Avraham (né Allen) and set him on the path to becoming a ba'al teshuvah and founder of "Chasidic rock." Flash-forward to 1979, as the Diaspora Yeshiva Band arrived for its gig in Los Angeles:

We were met at LAX by our friend, Olivia, whom we knew from Jerusalem. Olivia had become Lubavitch, and we had heard that she had married a widower rabbi with a big bunch of kids and a reputation for being a special guy. We would be staying for Shabbat with Rabbi Shlomo, Olivia, and the kids. The rabbi arrived as we were having lunch at their home. I immediately took inventory: Russian cap. Wire-rim glasses. Black T-shirt with glittering letters that read, "Schwartzie." Tight blue jeans. Moose antler belt buckle. Tzitzis a yard long. Holy cow! A special guy!! The most far-out rabbi I had beheld in my life with the sweetest and most unassuming presence, and funny as heck!

We were enjoying lunch and conversing with Schwartzie and Olivia and meeting all those beautiful kids, when for some reason, I began to think that the rabbi and I had crossed paths before. It became a strong feeling, and I apologetically interrupted the conversation to address my growing desire to figure it out. I asked Schwartzie the following questions:

Q: Where are you from?

A: Atlantic City, New Jersey. No, we never met there.

Q: Did we meet in Jerusalem?

A: No, I don't think so. And then . . .

Q: Were you in the Catskills in the summer of 1969?

A: Was there a Jew from New York who wasn't?

Q: Were you in Monticello in August, maybe the Woodstock weekend?

A: (He's staring at me.)

Q: That Sunday morning, were you visiting anyone at Monticello General Hospital?

A: He turned to Olivia and says, mystified, "I was visiting my brother in-law's friend whose ulcer had flared up."

I was breaking out in a sweat as I finally nervously asked, "Do you possibly remember speaking with some muddy Jewish hippie—in Yiddish?"

Schwartzie, in shock, put his hand up to his face and exclaimed, "Oy! You were so much skinnier then!"

I learned something very wonderful in that moment about the Divine Hand of G-d—that G-d gives a holy gift to those who are able to lead us home. It's called chein—grace. And Schwartzie had so much of it that the light produced in our meeting, ten years and ten thousand road miles earlier, never faded from my memory.

And then we made a l'chaim!

And then we made a l'chaim!

And then we made another l'chaim!

Thank you, Schwartzie, forever!

CHAPTER 42

WOODSTOCK 1994

When the twenty-fifth anniversary of Woodstock rolled around, two sets of organizers arranged concerts in upstate New York. The larger one, in Saugerties, on the west bank of the Hudson River, was designed as a money-making event, with paid admission and charges for food and drink; it attracted an estimated 350,000 people. An hour and a half southwest, on the site of the original 1969 Woodstock festival in Bethel, a free event was held the same weekend that drew about 30,000 people.

I was recruited by a few of my friends, including Rabbi Langer from San Francisco, to make a pilgrimage to the Woodstock reunion and do my Jewish shtick and connect with as many Jewish people as possible. We first went to the Saugerties concert but were thwarted by the corporate nature of the event, so we headed on to Bethel. "We got the boot," I told a member of one of the Bethel bands. We set up a table to blow shofar and give away thousands of apples because Rosh Hashanah was just days away. They said that it would cost us a thousand bucks to have our table there. We had a dozen boxes of apples and needed a command center to organize the distribution of all our apples.

"Don't have the extra thousand on hand?" the musician joked.

I said that we were not selling them. We were actually giving them away. I don't think anyone believed us at all. Especially when we could've sold each one for probably five bucks apiece.

Most of us know that the most important *mitzvah* of the Jewish New Year is to hear the *shofar* being blown. What most Jews *don't* know is that for an entire month before Rosh Hashanah, the *shofar* is sounded in the synagogue every morning.

How this happened: in the summer of 1994, I got a call from a great, creative rabbi in the Bay Area who said that five Chasidic rabbis were planning to attend Woodstock II. They were going to get on stage with ten thousand sweet apples and a shofar and explain in a short little sermon what all of it was about. Then they would blow the shofar and throw the ten thousand apples into the crowd. There would be many thousands of people there, but most of them would be able to get a bite. Somebody had kicked in all the expenses, so even if it didn't happen, we would still have a great time meeting all those people.

Off we went on a modern-day Chasidic adventure. We arrived in the Catskill Mountains in two cars with the cases of apples and one huge yeminite shofar.

After a really great Shabbat, on Sunday morning, we set out for the site, five rabbis and thousands of apples. There were police checkpoints in a cordon two miles square to stop all vehicles. We had big blessings upon us because every time we were stopped by the police, we just showed them all our apples and chanted our mantra: "These are the apples for the stage!" After a moment of quizzical stares, they waved us through to the stage.

Not so simple yet. There were two checkpoints to stop everyone from getting on stage.

Now we five rabbis were at the foot of the stage with our ten thousand apples. Suddenly, a burly man with a petite girlfriend hanging on his arm, neither of whom looked particularly Jewish, approached me, and without any hello or even a smile he said, "How much you want for the hat?"

I was wearing a baseball cap with a large "*chai*" on it. I didn't understand what a gentile wanted with a *chai* hat, but I didn't want to be too direct or confrontational and just come right out and ask him, "Are you Jewish?" So, I said, "What's your Jewish name?"

The dude looked at me for a minute as if he were trying to remember. Meanwhile, his little girlfriend pipes up proudly with, "My Jewish name is Pesha Dvosha!"

OK, so *she's* Jewish. At that moment, I noticed that among the many badges hanging around his neck was an "ALL ACCESS" pass. That meant that he was a somebody. He turned out to be the roadie for Richie Havens, a real somebody super-celeb who had played the first Woodstock. Then this *bulvan*, covered with tattoos, asked the fateful question, "What are you doing here?" I pointed to the cases of apples and explained that Rosh

Hashanah was in two weeks and that the custom is to eat sweet apples in order to be blessed with a sweet new year. He said, "Follow me." I told him I had a group of another four rabbis. He motioned that we should all follow him onto the stage.

There we all were, backstage: five Chasidic rabbis and ten thousand apples. We were having a really great time, peeking out from the stage at the enthusiastic audience. However, the main objective hadn't been accomplished yet. We needed to get the mic and communicate our important message to all those gentiles (and a few Jews).

Suddenly, there was a big tumult. A very large man, naked to the waist, totally muscle bound, high on a very bad trip (angel dust?), somehow broke through both security checkpoints and got onto the stage.

The head of security, backed up by two humongous, unsmiling "Blue Meanies," walked right up to the intruder and confronted him directly. At this point, I was thinking I should perhaps jump off the stage, as it seemed certain that violence was about to ensue. And I don't like the sight of blood. But, strange as it may seem, the man seemed to reflect for a moment and then slowly turned around and walked off the stage.

I wondered why I was supposed to see that and what significance it had for me. So I walked up to the head of security. He looked at me quizzically, like what do *you* want? I said, "I saw what you did—in that potentially dangerous situation. You stopped the whole thing before it went anywhere." He smiled at me. At that instant, it crossed my mind that he's Israeli, so I rattled off in speedy Hebrew, "Where have you been all my life; I'm looking for you under the benches by candlelight!"

He smiled even larger and hugged me very strongly and affectionately. Then he said, "Dude, I didn't understand a word you said; I'm an Italian from the Bronx, but you are beautiful, and I love you!" Then he asked me the same fateful question: "What are you doing here?"

I pointed to the cases of apples and showed him the gargantuan yeminite shofar and explained that we were rabbis and wanted to give the apples to the crowd and blow the ram's horn and bless everyone with a sweet new year.

He asked, "How long does that all have to take?"

I answered, four and a half minutes. And he said, "OK, you'll go on between Arlo Guthrie (that'd be Woody's son, who's actually Jewish) and Richie Havens."

And that's what happened. It was the largest congregation I had ever spoken to, before or since!

We blew the shofar and threw out the ten thousand apples into the crowd. They loved it!

Mission accomplished!

*   *   *

At that same concert, David Lazerson was preparing to take the stage with Avraham Rosenblum, founder of the Diaspora Yeshiva Band that originated "Chasidic rock" in the late 1970's who I met in '69 in that hospital.

David was anxious about playing their Jewish-themed rock-bluegrass fusion at Woodstock II. A hundred questions ran through my mind. "How would this massive crowd react to their music? Would anything with a Jewish flavor and vibe go over here? What if they didn't like them? One underlying question was, of course, how fast could we run?"

David continues the story in his words:

I'll never forget how this rumor ran wild through the crowd that Saturday night. Seeing Rabbis Langer and Schwartzie, along with my close friend and fellow rocker Simcha Gottlieb, with their really long, funky beards, everyone started talking about how ZZ Top was here in Bethel to play! Spontaneous cheers erupted through the crowd. "Awesome!" some shouted. "Wooohooo!" others cheered. Still others yelled out things like, "Oh, yeah!" and, "All right!" Now things were going to really get rocking, they thought.

The two fearless rabbis took the stage Saturday night, a good two hours after Shabbat went out. This is going to be really interesting, I thought to myself. It was only a matter of minutes before the crowd found out that these two were not actually the hard-rockin' front-men of ZZ Top. I looked around for a place to hide in case things got ugly.

Schwartzie smiled, patted me on the back, and added, "Divine Providence strikes . . . we're meant to be right here right now! So let's see what the Boss has in store for us."

Schwartzie and Langer strode boldly to center stage and took a couple of microphones. Both smiled broadly to the huge crowd. They were now in the spotlight as a hush came over the countryside in Bethel. I don't remember exactly who said what because, quite frankly, they both looked very much alike to me, especially wearing their long kapotas and black hats.

"Saugerties," one of the rabbis said, "proves the power of the almighty dollar."

"Bethel," the other added, "proves the power of the Almighty!"

To my utter surprise, the crowd roared and applauded in approval.

"We've shown right here in Bethel," they continued, "that we can all get along, enjoy each other's company, and help each other out."

I couldn't help but marvel at this totally hip and outrageously cool Chasidic duo. Schwartzie and Langer seemed to have this magic emanating from their very beings. Many in the crowd, more than I could ever count, came up to speak to them afterward. Some came just to get a closer look at these two holy, unusual, yet very friendly, down-to-earth rabbis.

They spoke to the thirty-thousand-plus people, and by the time their ten minutes of glory were over, they had wished everyone a happy, healthy upcoming New Year and had blown the shofar right on the stage that would later host Arlo Guthrie, Melanie, and other performers who had, in fact, played Woodstock twenty-five years earlier. It would also host Avraham and me, but not until Sunday morning.

Their stage appearance gave me a needed booster shot. Later that night, we held a sort of impromptu mini-fabrengen. Schwartzie and Langer shared some stories and

wisdom (and a few l'chaims) with Simcha, Avraham, and me.

They touched on this notion of how we simply have to be who we are: no pretenses, no need for false humility or compromises, no matter where we are—even if we find ourselves on center stage at Woodstock. "Just be who you are," Schwartzie later reminded me. "We don't have to be pushy . . . just stay warm and open. If we're a light, others will automatically come closer." I no longer feared taking that stage myself. Seeing how these two incredible rabbis related so remarkably well to the throngs of people was a clear demonstration to me that there was absolutely no need for worry. We all drank another quick l'chaim, and Schwartzie added, "Besides, as an emissary of the Rebbe, the tzaddik yesod olam (righteous one, foundation of the world), you go with the Rebbe's strength and blessings."

But a big part of our success was watching Schwartzie and Langer in action. I will never forget how they stood on that stage at Woodstock and, with this rare combination of confidence and humility, related to each and every person in that crowd. Despite looking very Chasidic, their message of love, respect, and living life with purpose resonated with one and all.

Before we left Woodstock, the rabbis told me to "carry on and rock the world."

CHAPTER 43

THE MOSH PIT

Matisyahu, the suburban kid from White Plains, New York, who joined
Chabad Lubavitch in 2001 and broke through as a star with his brand of
"Chasidic reggae" and hip-hop a couple of years later, was still affiliated
with Chabad in Brooklyn when, fascinated by his backstory, I caught up
with him in concert in 2006.

I had been hearing about this talented Jewish boy from Brooklyn,
from a non-Orthodox home, who got into reggae music as a kid. Having a
yiddishe kop and talent, he got pretty good at it.

At age twenty-two, Matisyahu hooked up with Chabad after a period
of moving in that direction. After he finished his yeshiva studies, got
married to another ba'al teshuvah, and had a kid, he recognized his responsibility. But what to do?

He started doing what he knew—performing reggae. And the rest, as
they say, is history. He went from $5,000 to $50,000 per performance in
less than two years.

I'd heard that Matisyahu performed in full Chasidic regalia, with the
standard "penguin" look: white shirt, black suit and fedora, with tzitzis
hangin'/danglin'/dancin' out from underneath his shirt. He made it onto
national radio and then MTV. And I heard that instead of playing for
Hadassah and the National Council of Jewish Women et al., he was getting
gigs in non-Jewish bars across America, in places like Texas.

This I wanted to see. So I did.

I went to catch his act at a kind of sleazy club on "Hollyweird" Boulevard. (For some reason, sleaziness never stopped me.) When he appeared on stage, he looked, unimpressively, like every Talmud Torah teacher in Brooklyn. He began to sing to an enthusiastic crowd of about four hundred, mostly reggae aficionados, plus a few curious Jews like me. He was OK.

After less than five minutes, he took off his black Chasidic fedora and sailed it into the crowd. They went wild! After another four minutes, he took off his black suit jacket and tossed it on a chair on the stage. The immediate reaction of shrill, piercing screams reminded me of when I was a kid and saw Elvis on the *Ed Sullivan Show* for the first time.

About fifteen minutes into the show, he paused, got a strange gleam in his eye, and slowly backed up on the stage, away from the audience. Then, while the loud music continued, he started running toward the front of the stage, but instead of stopping, he leaped off the stage into the audience.

I was shocked. I had never seen that before. (Dylan *never* did that!)

They called it "body surfing." At this point, the screams were just so loud that I had to go.

By the time Matisyahu came to Santa Monica to sign a contract with Yahoo Music, he had heard of Olivia and me, and he asked to stay at our house for the night to avoid the mobs at the hotels. When we broke bread, he washed for the bread prior to our lunch. He asked for salt to dip his bread in, which is a Kabbalistic custom. I realized he's the real deal. He was more religious than Olivia and I combined were. We shmoozed and hung out, and he sang with my grandkids, a real sweetie. After lunch, his stretch limo and driver came to our home to take him to the studio. It was a short while after that when he became famous again, especially in the Orthodox communities, when he removed his beard.

I choose to follow *The Ethics of the Fathers*, which states, "Don't judge an individual until you're standing in his shoes." Matisyahu was unable to attend my seventieth birthday bash at the El Rey Theater, but he did give me a shout-out via video from Sao Paulo, Brazil.

* * *

I always had an affinity for the Grateful Dead.

My friend laid on me four $150 tickets to the Grateful Dead at the Forum one Saturday night. I gave away three and jumped on one.

It was a great show (even though old timers like me could feel the absence of Jerry). Because the Sabbath ended so late and I was way out in the San Fernando Valley for a bar mitzvah, I got to the Great Forum right after the first set.

Actually, that was really great, because I was cruising around the food concessions during the intermission, and with no effort, I picked up seven Jews. That's not counting all the high-fives and smiling Jewish faces that lit up when they saw me, although they weren't immediately sure until they saw the "Chai" hat. I've never been greeted that warmly by Jews, even at my own free High Holiday services.

Then I was seated for the second set, settled in with a humongous capacity crowd of thousands, enjoying the eye candy of the multitudinous array of flowing tie-dyed and rainbow clothes.

Suddenly, I had a fleeting thought that the holiday of Shavuot was around the corner, and how did all this relate to that one-time, all-important event in Jewish history: G-d's giving us the Torah on Mt. Sinai, complete with thunder and lightning?

Just then, the crowd started screaming wildly (a signal that the Dead were going to play an old favorite), and the audience began to sing the words so loudly that I could decipher all the lyrics. It was a song I was familiar with but couldn't place until the crowd got *really* loud singing "Fire on the mountain…"

There it was: my connection to the Decalogue.

"Fire on the mountain"—of SINAI.

I've had many more experiences and relationships with musicians and actors, as many of their managers and agents would come to my Kabbalah class: Bob Dylan, Adam Sandler, Richard Dreyfuss, Elliott Gould, and Jane Fonda to name a few.

Let's move on though . . .

CHAPTER 44

SWAMI SATCHIDANANDA

Thank G-d, I had a part in many people coming back to Judaism, sometimes from very far away.

There was the Dutch man whose parents had hidden the fact they were Jewish until he found out as a teen and had himself circumcised at twenty-one. I trained him for the bar mitzvah he had at age thirty-four and stayed friendly with him until he made aliyah a few years later.

There was the JuBu (Jewish Buddhist) I met at a conference, the daughter of the owner of the only kosher-style deli in Salt Lake City, who was taken aback when I asked her to light Shabbat candles. "Can I still do it?" she asked, bursting into tears when I said yes.

Then there was the man in his sixties, reared as a Southern Baptist in the deep South, who was brought to one of our Chai Center Passover seders. Three weeks earlier, his mother, on her deathbed, had told him that her mother had been born Jewish, so she was a Jew, and so was he. I called upon him to read during the seder, and he lit up like a light bulb.

And there was this young seeker I met in 2008:

At one of my morning classes in Israel, I only had twelve people, so even though I never do it, I asked all these new people, including the new couple, to introduce themselves by saying their names and where they were from. With a proud smile, the young woman said her name was Dvora, and he said (a little self-consciously) that he was Krishna from Ukiah, California. That told me a lot about this very spiritual, *eidel*, sweet, long-haired twenty-three-year-old. Not a lot of people live in Ukiah, a gorgeous place in Mendocino County, except for old hippies left over from the '60s, which is why he had a Hindu name like Krishna—he got it from his aging hippie parents when they were younger hippies.

Krishna actually was fascinated when he learned in my class that Judaism has deep roots in mysticism and meditation. He and Dvora had been living together for about a year, and she was pushing the Jewish (but not Orthodox) agenda, so he wasn't a complete stranger. The woman was sweet, but I could tell that he was deep and extremely bright. He shared that he felt bad about not having a Jewish name. That was a red flag. It meant he didn't have a proper bris, because boys get a Jewish name at the bris. Later, he confirmed that his parents were old hippies, but he still had a *bubbe* who was ninety-two and lived in Culver City, right next door to us in Los Angeles.

I saw that he had a connection to spirituality of the Eastern variety, so in class, I started using examples from the different Eastern faith movements to illustrate ideas. Each time I mentioned another guru, I noted his reaction. Finally, I mentioned how I used to teach Hebrew to the head of the Integral Yoga Institute of Hollywood and actually went to hear Swami Satchidananda at (of all places) Hollywood Temple Beth El. I told the class how two thousand Jews came to a shul that night to hear this tall, imposing, gorgeous guru with sparkling eyes, long hair, and a long salt-and-pepper beard. It worked. Krishna lit up, disarmed himself, and accepted me as a comrade. He became visibly relaxed, enough to share more personal details.

The plot thickened: his dad wasn't Jewish and was a follower of Swami Satchidananda; he's the one who had named the kid Krishna. The really bad news was that because his folks were hippies, they were vegetarians, too, because they didn't want to spill blood. And they chose a "natural" lifestyle, so not only had the parents not had a proper bris for Krishna—but also Krishna was uncircumcised, period. Dvora became a bit embarrassed and started asking me to convince him to have a bris! Krishna promised to bring his beloved *bubbe* to our Shabbat table in Los Angeles. That's when we'll really get him and convince him to spill his blood.

CHAPTER 45

AN ARMENIAN CHRISTIAN AMONG THE ORTHODOX

Our large home, with heated pool, Jacuzzi, and open (but strictly kosher) kitchen, has served, for many years, as a party house for teens and twenty-somethings when the owners (the Schwartzes) are away in Israel every summer. Call it a private "City of Refuge;" it's been a bed-and-breakfast (plus other meals) for many kids at many levels of Jewish practice.

We got home from Israel one August and joined the ongoing festival taking place on our backyard patio. About twenty young people were sitting at a table laden with beverages and munchies. Everyone was Jewish at various levels. Some were dropouts from ultra-Orthodox Chasidic families, with rabbis for fathers, and some were just "regular" young Jews, mostly children of people originally from the East Coast, kids who grew up with a love for Israel and Jewish tradition.

Suddenly, there was a brief lull in everyone's conversation. It was one of those moments when all the kids had been talking with raised voices so they could be heard over all the other voices, but they all finished a sentence at the same time, so anyone who spoke up would be heard loud and clear. In the brief silence, a simple, straightforward question in a loud, clearly articulated voice rang out as if it were on a PA system:

"What's a mezuzah?"

All eyes turned to the good-looking, long-haired, twenty-year-old actor with the non-Jewish surname. He asked the question as if he had never heard the word *mezuzah* before in his entire life. And he never had.

Out came his story: His biological mother was Jewish, but she married an Armenian Christian man, and the kid had been brought up in the Armenian Orthodox community, eventually with his dad and an Armenian stepmother. He actually spoke Armenian. Obviously, he never had a bar mitzvah; he'd never even stepped inside a temple.

A year before I met him, he had started hanging out with a Jewish crowd. He had no clue what they were talking about half the time, but they were cool and a great deal of fun, and they liked their religion and practiced it.

When his new friends heard that he had a Jewish mother, they showed him how to observe the biblical commandment of tefillin. They also introduced him to the Orthodox 'hood in Pico-Robertson and its various watering holes.

When all the assorted Jews on our patio heard him tell his story, they all wanted to adopt him. He got invites to at least four different Shabbat gatherings.

Of course, we invited him to the young adults' "Dinner for 60 Strangers" for ages twenty-one to thirty-nine. He's already up for going on his first-ever trip to Israel via Birthright.

I was super-excited. I'm not sure how fast our circumstantial hero was on a fast track to a black hat, but he certainly seemed to be on fire to know about his (previously submerged) quintessential identity. Greg eventually moved into our home and grabbed a bed. He even spoke at one of our galas in 2015.

Phyllis Pollack *eulogized Schwartzie after his passing.*

My parents were atheists. I had a bat mitzvah only because it would have looked bad to the neighbors if I hadn't. But afterward, my parents forbade me to have any further religious education, despite my begging. The past generations of my family in Europe had been very highly observant, but I knew nothing about my religion. I had no idea even that you were supposed to light Shabbat candles until I was in my late twenties.

It seemed that most of the Orthodox Jews I ran into were not accepting of me, to say the least. It was like I was "not Jewish enough." I felt uncomfortable around some Orthodox people because of those experiences.

Then I met Schwartzie thirty years ago at UCLA. I don't know why I was even there. Anyway, Schwartzie approached me and asked me whether I was Jewish. I said, "Yeah," and I went to see him at the university several times. After he gave me some facts from the Torah, he had me absolutely convinced me the Torah was real. What he told me was life-changing. I still remember how he convinced me, what the words were that he told me.

Schwartzie loved all Jews. He was able to communicate with your Jewish soul—and to help you find it. That was his greatest gift to me. It did not matter that I was not Orthodox. I was a Jew.

Schwartzie found my Jewish soul, which I never would have found on my own.

For his giving me that gift, I will always remain eternally grateful to him.

*   *   *

Chana Schoenberg wrote a letter to Schwartzie on his seventieth birthday.

I am here today in Ramat Bet Shemesh, wearing a wig, challah dough rising, prayer book by my side, all because of Shlomo.

There are too many things to recount and relate. But a few things stand out:

He was the one who "brought me back" when we lived in West Los Angeles. We are talking about 1969–70—oy! He never gave up on me, although he always reminded me that I was a very tough case.

I wanted him to meet Baba Ram Dass—a nice Jewish boy, Richard Alpert—and appear at a concert with him. Shlomo gave me a little talk on why that wasn't such a good idea. He didn't preach; he graciously explained and enlightened.

He was instrumental in conducting my father's funeral at Eden Memorial with sensitivity and kindness in 1972. I had just returned from a one-year stint in Israel on my way to Katmandu. He explained why Katmandu wouldn't be a good idea. I fought him, of course—but in the end I didn't go there.

Shlomo plucked me out of the Yoga Institute at 26th and Broadway in New York City. He insisted that I go to 770 in Brooklyn and stay with lovely people over Shabbat. I was suspicious, but after a few hours that Shabbat, the seed was planted, and there was no going back, much to my dismay!

He is a special man with a special mission at which he has excelled immensely. The proof is in the pudding, as they say: he helped jump-start us—another religious family with offspring!

CHAPTER 46

SHABBAT 1000 IN AUSTRIA

A few years ago, I was asked to be the guest speaker for "Shabbat 1000" at the University of Texas at Austin. The Shabbat 1000 folks would serve a thousand Jewish students a free, full-course Shabbat dinner. There was no formal Jewish service. Everyone showed up on time for the free meal. The only requirement was to be quiet for the rabbi's fifteen-minute sermon.

Because of Shabbat, no one used a microphone, so a guest rabbi had to come because the local rabbi in Austin couldn't belt out his speech loudly enough for everyone to hear. Because I have a very loud voice, I was invited to be the guest rabbi. I distilled my best stories of nineteen years on campus down to an exciting fifteen minutes, with an attitude that was the opposite of uptight.

At that dinner, I met a young, good-looking Australian guy who was working in Jewish outreach. We hung out for the weekend and became fast friends. I came home to Los Angeles and told my wife, Olivia, that the Aussie was destined for greatness in Jewish outreach.

Six years later, this young man, now married with two kids, had founded the European Center for Jewish Students (ECJS). He planned a New Year's Eve weekend in Vienna, Austria, at the prestigious Hilton, and almost three hundred students registered, at $210 per person. A few came from Paris and London. And many came from Warsaw, Budapest, Moldova, Brussels, Oslo, and cities in Italy. Most of the rabbis in Europe were pretty straight and boring, so my Aussie friend Yossi hired me to be a sort of rabbinical emcee.

Between Thursday night and Sunday morning, we were able to meet dozens of individuals, ages eighteen to twenty-six, and hear their personal stories. Olivia was just sitting and listening . . . and crying. There was the smashing blonde from Warsaw who worked for Polish television. Two years earlier, when she was twenty-two, her mother had become seriously ill and told her that she was Jewish and gave her a necklace with a Jewish star that had belonged to her grandmother, the blonde's great-grandmother. Since then, this young woman had been passionately driven to find out about her Judaism and had started to get involved in the religion.

Then there was the student from Geneva whose mom had married a Jew and had begun to take on some traditions and drag her hubby to temple. The student developed an interest when she was fifteen and had converted formally at age eighteen. She went on Birthright at twenty and was now twenty-two and hungry for any tidbit about Torah and practice. There were also two roommates from Italy who were clueless and had come to party for New Year's, but Olivia zeroed in on them, and by Sunday morning at the grand farewell, they were almost crying about having to part from their new rabbi.

Nowhere in my life had I seen so many young women drink so much hard liquor.

On Friday evening during the meal, I went into the lobby for a few minutes. I saw a family sitting together, an older man with his wife and their two adult children. As I passed by wearing my kipah, the man gave me the most beautiful smile. It certainly seemed like he wanted to say hello. But in Europe, that's just not done—nobody approaches strangers and begins a conversation. Because I'm not from Europe and don't abide by its rules, I approached them, and his smile grew even broader. He was ecstatic that I had come over. He spoke Yiddish, and I got the whole story.

He was originally from Vienna. In 1938, when he was sixteen years old and the Nazis took over Vienna, both he and his father were arrested for the crime of being Jewish and sent to Dachau. Luckily, the war had not yet been declared; it was pre-Final Solution. Because he was only sixteen, he was sent back home. His father came home after four months. At that point, they fled to Brazil.

This man was now in his seventies, and it was the first time he had returned to Vienna to visit. He was a guest at the Hilton and was in the lobby watching the parade of beautiful Jewish college kids traipsing around. He told me he would be content sitting there for many more hours just to take it all in. Of course we shlepped him and his family into the ballroom and made them eat the amazing Shabbat banquet meal with all of us. He then told me, crying, that tonight was the first Shabbat meal he had had since leaving Vienna sixty years earlier.

After all the programs had ended, I went to the lobby after midnight and saw about one hundred people from our group shmoozing. Many of the guys, still wearing kipot, were smoking and yammering on cell phones. Even though it was Shabbat, I loved it. The roar, the deafening sound of conversation, was sweeter than music, more exciting than a rock concert.

Saturday night was New Year's Eve, and the five-star Hilton's Grand Ballroom was the scene of a formal ball. Yossi brought a seven-piece band from Amsterdam. The many bar stations were mobbed, and drinks were expensive. The resourceful students brought their own bottles and, as they got to know one another, went up to their rooms for brief intermissions from dancing to drink more and "get to know" their partners even better. At the crucial moment of 11:45 p.m., when folks were jockeying for position for the traditional kiss, the band suddenly stopped. I had the unforgettable honor of going up on stage and speaking for two minutes (*maximum*) and then lighting the Chanukah menorah. Only 10 percent of the young people knew "*Maoz tzur*," but everybody was up for the New Year's-Chanukah experience.

About 3:30 a.m., when the band stopped and I left, there were still nearly one hundred students at the tables in the Grand Ballroom hanging out.

Yossi, who had been working in Europe for the previous two years, realized what was needed for the event to be successful. He needed a wild and crazy rabbi (a Jewish Steve Martin) who was not like any of the rabbis these young European students had experienced. He remembered bar-hopping with me back in Austin, Texas, looking for Jewish students. He remembered my fifteen-minute sermon that held the attention of the thousand students. My wife and I came to Vienna to excite and inspire. In the end, it was we who were inspired. We came away deeply moved by the students.

CHAPTER 47

WHAT KIND OF JOB IS RABBI FOR A NICE JEWISH BOY?

Have you ever heard of a Reform ba'al teshuvah?

Stephen S. Wise Temple is among the largest synagogues west of the Mississippi River, with five or six rabbis and more than two thousand members. It sits on a huge, beautiful campus at the top of a mountain in the wealthy Bel Air neighborhood of Los Angeles. It's a Reform congregation, so it's been known to set out pepperoni pizza for its religious school kids. I'm friendly with Nate Lam, who's been cantor there forever.

Nate used to hold an adult *b'nai mitzvah* class every year. He would work with dozens of Jews who had never had a bar or bat mitzvah. One year in the early 1980s, he had about seventy students in the class, the youngest twenty-five and the oldest sixty-five. He asked me to be a guest lecturer for the class. I did, and I was really "on" that day. I spoke for forty-five minutes, and then there was a very lively Q&A session.

After the class, the twenty-five-year-old, a nice-looking young man, came up to me and was serious about some questions. He said he had grown up in a very assimilated, barely Jewish family that never went to temple, even on Yom Kippur, which is why he'd never had a bar mitzvah.

He'd passed the bar two years earlier and had been working in his father's law firm ever since. His life seemed to be cruising down Easy Street, but at some point he had been bitten by the bug of transcendental experience and was more interested in spirituality than in making money. In short, he was miserable staring down the tunnel of a law career, and he actually wanted to become a rabbi!

Of course, my response was, "What kind of job is that for a nice Jewish boy?"

I then asked my new friend Jeffrey to engage in my favorite sport: "doing lunch." He started learning with me regularly, everything from Torah to *Tanya,* with a *l'chaim* when we finished the hour. Obviously, we developed a close personal relationship.

Early in 1984, I took him to visit Yeshiva University's modern Orthodox seminary, and he also checked out the Conservative movement's University of Judaism (now American Jewish University) and Reform's Hebrew Union College. I encouraged him to go to Yeshiva, but he chose Reform and enrolled at HUC. I was OK with that. I figured it would be good for the Jews if we had a man on the inside, so to speak.

After graduation, Jeffrey got a job at Emanuel Synagogue, the largest temple in Sydney, Australia, as associate rabbi. After some years, the senior rabbi became emeritus, and Rabbi Jeffrey Kamins became the senior rabbi at Emanuel.

His *rebbetzin* was a slightly older Jewish woman named Bobette from Shreveport, Louisiana (as he liked to say: "before the term 'cougar' was invented"). I visited them in 1990. Back then, they didn't keep kosher, but all I wanted was a Danish and a cup of coffee. But they were new in town and didn't know where the kosher bakery was.

Still, Rabbi Kamins' message to his new congregation before his first High Holidays in Sydney was all about some of the fundamental mitzvahs. He advocated hardcore commandments, such as wearing tefillin, keeping kosher, Torah study, and mikvah practice for married couples. He had become what I'd hoped he'd become: our man on the inside, that is, traditional Judaism's representative in a progressive Jewish institution.

Senior Rabbi, Jeffrey B. Kamins
Emanuel Synagogue, Sydney Australia

FINAL DAYS

CHAPTER 48

TWO HEARTS, TWO SOULS: FINAL CLASS AT THE GROVE

Schwartzie's physical decline began in 2011, when he suffered a broken hip and minor head trauma in an automobile accident. After surgery, he developed a rare condition that caused excess bone to grow at the repaired pelvis. That condition, heterotopic ossification, caused him serious pain for the rest of his life and disrupted his daily activities: he could no longer drive, he had to use a cane, and it was difficult for him to get in or out of a chair.

After two and a half years, the excess bone stopped growing and Schwartzie hoped to improve his physical condition with surgery. But just before the surgery, he noticed a lump on his face, near his jaw, and reported that his ear hurt. The surgeon, fearing an ear infection, canceled the surgery.

Antibiotics knocked out the ear infection, but the lump remained, and in 2014, Schwartzie was diagnosed with multiple myeloma, a cancer of the blood that inhibits the production of red blood cells, causes anemia, and attacks white blood cells, compromising the immune system.

The cancer added systemic illness to his mobility issues, which could not be corrected. He also developed cataracts that blurred his vision and made reading difficult. Nevertheless, Schwartzie continued to learn and teach until just a few weeks before his passing on Wednesday, February 8, 2017.

"Even from the accident, in the beginning, he would just learn. He would just sit and learn," said his wife, Olivia. "People would come if he felt OK; if he didn't feel OK, then he didn't. It was up and down. The thing that he loved the most was learning and teaching other people."

Schwartzie's last series of lectures took place before an audience in a meeting space at the Grove shopping center in Los Angeles. Even given his difficulties in sitting, moving, and reading, "he prepared for those Grove lectures as if he were a young rookie rabbi right out of rabbinical college," his son Mendel said.

He delivered the talk below, using Deuteronomy 6:5—"You shall love haShem your G-d with all your heart, with all your soul, and with all your being"—as his text, on his 71st birthday on the Hebrew calendar, 7 Kislev 5777, barely two months before his death.

Take the most important sentence [the *Sh'ma*] and the most important prayer in our religion. Look at the phrase that's translated, "with all your heart." It should say, *V'ahavta et-haShem Elohecha b'chol livcha:* love G-d with all your heart. It doesn't say that; it says *l'vavcha,* which means *l'vavot shelcha,* the plural, your *hearts.* You didn't know you had two, huh?

You've got two, not one. This could be the most important thing in the Kabbalah, that you don't have one heart, but two. One heart is a natural heart; the other is passion. What's the second that I'm pushing through? What's the second way to love? Soul.

I was a rabbi at UCLA for twenty years. For twenty years, incoming freshmen all had the same major. What was that? Psychology. They're desperate to know who they are. They are eighteen, nineteen, twenty, and twenty-one years old. They want to know, "What makes me tick? Why do I react the way I do? Why does this person do something freely, whereas another person doesn't? Why do you push my buttons? Why are things great one day and not the other? Why do I love my mother and still fight with her? I call her and then I hang up on her, and I'm angry and fighting with my mother! Why?" Especially because in the Ten Commandments, it says to honor your mother for long life. You can deduce that if you don't, the result could be a short life, G-d forbid.

Most people think that a human being is a composition comprising body and soul. Wrong. If that's the case, then we are all spiritual schizophrenics, because we have these two levels of consciousness pulling us. The other side of the same coin. I love my significant other; I hate my significant other. I love you, but I hate when you do that. I hate when you say that. I hate when you behave like that, but I love you. I'm staying with you forever; you're my soulmate.

There are two souls, not one. The first soul enters; when it enters depends on whom you ask, but, of course, in Kabbalah, it's conception. Boom, a heart. That's the first soul. The second soul comes about later. For a female, what age does the second soul come in? Twelve and a day for a girl. For a male, thirteen and a day. That's what bar mitzvah is all about. Don't rip off the Jewish woman. It's not thirteen; you're robbing her of a year of her life in which she can do things—that she can bring down G-dliness and can attach herself to the almighty Infinite G-d. It's twelve for a girl and thirteen for a boy.

The two souls, it's not that we're spiritual schizoids. It's that we have this double level of consciousness. One is called the natural soul, through what comes naturally. The other is called the holy soul. But what the Torah is requiring of us is to love with both. Love the Lord with all your souls, in the plural. Natural souls do what comes naturally. You hit me, and I'll hit you back. The divine soul, the holy soul is . . . well, let me just set it up for you.

You push the pause button; there's a two-second pause button. Think about that. Let it take hold; contemplate. Push the two-second pause button, and whether you're thinking a thought or you want to say something or you want to do something, think, which soul is motivated to think that thought or say those words or do that deed? Someone insults you in public, and you think of a comeback. She's going to swear she didn't want to be born when I finish giving her the rejoinder and getting her back after what she did to me. Is that the natural soul or the holy soul?

Well, it can't be the holy, divine, G-dly soul. It's got to be that natural—rational even, logical even—soul. But loving G-d with your two souls, that's the commandment. Not just with your holy soul; it's easy to love G-d with your connection to G-d. The holy, divine, G-dly soul. But it's important to love G-d even with your natural soul—you could even call it the animal soul because it's animal instinct, animal urge. That's what comes naturally. But that's not what the Torah requires of us. The Torah is telling us to love G-d not only with your holy soul, but also with your natural soul.

Meaning, push the two-second pause button and think: which soul is motivating me to say these words to that person or to do this deed to myself even?

Emotions, it's called the ten soul powers. Three direct powers and seven emotions. How many times does a man wrap a strap between his elbow and his wrist, how many times? Seven. Seven between elbow and wrist. Seven times. What's the Kabbalistic meditation when you're wrapping those seven coils between your elbow and your wrist? The meditation is: I want to bind up all my seven emotions with a power higher than myself. What's the Kabbalistic meditation when you're winding three coils before the seven that make it ten soul powers? On your bicep or the seat of your power of your hand. The three intellect powers: you can use your intellect to strike back at somebody if he or she hurts you, or you can use your intellect to find a cure for cancer. It depends what you do with it. There are things that are neither fish nor fowl. They're what you make of them.

Think about time. Time is what you do with it. You can kill time. If you do that, you're a murderer; you're murdering yourself. Time, food, intellect, emotions. Love for your significant other, your wife, is a mitzvah. Love for someone else's wife is not a mitzvah. Ten powers in your soul, subdivided into three and seven. Three intellect powers, seven emotions. There's a lot to talk about.

The intellect soul is born in the head, and the natural soul is born in the heart, but once they become defined, they have some substance. They have action or thought through a deed they want to perform, then the action or thought becomes a reality. It goes from a general soul to actual heart, which depends on your actually doing something, whether it's thought, speech, or deed.

Now, I just want to say one last thing in conclusion. The Kabbalah says that on your birthday—tonight is my birthday—your star shines the brightest, which means you have the power on your Jewish soul birthday to bless people. I want to bless everybody here and everybody who is listening. G-d should give you the blessings of the highest success, beyond your highest estimate of what you think should be your success. G-d bless you all.

CHAPTER 49

GLUE YOURSELF TO A MOSES IN THIS GENERATION: FINAL TALK

The following is an excerpt from a teaching Schwartzie delivered on Chanukah in December 2016. This was to be the last talk he ever gave.

Rabbi Isaac Luria, who lived to be only thirty-eight years old, founded a school of Kabbalah teachings during the sixteenth century that are what most people think of when they think of Kabbalah. He said there are 600,000 meanings to each sentence in the Bible, but generally we can divide those meanings into two: the revealed Torah and the hidden Torah.

Revealed Torah, everybody can read. To study the hidden Torah, though, according to Rabbi Luria, there must be some preconditions, prerequisites: you should be married; you should be at least forty years old; you should be an unbelievable, prolific scholar of the revealed Torah, of the Bible, the Mishnah, the Talmud. Then, finally, you can understand what the Moses of our generation is saying.

The idea behind that sort of thing is, if you find *that* Moses, a real live tzaddik, then it connects you to one of the 613 commandments in the Torah that most people don't really talk about. We know about the commandments of putting on tefillin, keeping Shabbat, not eating *treif*—the concrete stuff about what to do and what not to do. But there's a commandment most people don't pay attention to; it's two words in the Torah.

The two words are *uvo*, "and in him," with "him" meaning Moses or the tzaddik of the time, *tidbakun*. What does *devek* mean? Glue. So, one of the commandments in the Torah is *uvo tidbakun*: glue yourself to the Moses of a generation. It doesn't matter who it is. Your Moses. The one whom you respect, the one who understands you.

All the princes of the twelve tribes had the psychic ability to understand any member of their respective tribes. But only one person had the psychic ability, the *ruach hakodesh*, the holy spirit, to understand all the tribes. And that was Moshe *Rabbeinu*. People came by, and he told them what their past lives were. So, we know how to put on tefillin. We know how to dwell in the sukkah. We know how to wear tzitzit. But how do you glue yourself to G-d?

For all the nuts-and-bolts mitzvahs, we have a *Shulchan Aruch*, a code of Jewish law, that says how to carry out each mitzvah, what the minimum requirements are, or how many ounces of matzah you have to stuff down your throat to make sure you did that commandment in the Bible. People have all kinds of measuring sticks and rods. But how do you fulfill a commandment of gluing yourself to G-d? For that, we look to the Talmud. The *Gemara* says that one of the ways to glue yourself to G-d is to read the Torah of the tzaddik: his commentary, his explanation of verses in the Torah. That's essential and important.

For some Jews, that tzaddik was the Lubavitcher Rebbe. There was a Russian Jew when there still was communism, when the Jews weren't allowed to leave Russia for seventy years. A guy smuggled out a letter to the Rebbe in New York and said, "I became a ba'al teshuvah. And, Lubavitcher Rebbe, I'm reading your Torah and your explanations of Rashi and all the Torah that you've written. But I have never seen you personally, face to face, and I don't have that experience. I want to be connected to you. I want to glue myself to the Moses of our generation, who I think is you. How do I do that?" And the Rebbe answered him through a smuggled letter, "Read my Torah, because that's coming from my soul, the highest level."

There is a thing about visiting the grave of a tzaddik, the tomb of a tzaddik. What do you call Orthodox sightseeing in Israel? Grave hopping. I mean, that's what people do who know who these people were, who were these scholars, these mystics, what kind of light they brought into the world. It's said that when you read aloud the Torah explanation of a tzaddik, the lips of that tzaddik, even if he passed away a thousand years ago, are moving in his grave, saying the same words that you're saying. That's another way to glue yourself to the tzaddik.

Just this week, I saw a video of Rabbi Shlomo Carlebach saying the eulogy for the late Lubavitcher Rebbe, and he ended with the words, "There was never a Rebbe like the late Lubavitcher Rebbe, and there never again will be one like him." Even knowing that, we can still find a tzaddik. We can choose a tzaddik, connect to and glue ourselves to a tzaddik.

So, go and find a tzaddik. Everybody should have great success in picking a tzaddik to connect to and become glued to.

CHAPTER 50

GROWING UP SCHWARTZIE

To everyone, our father was Schwartzie. To us, he was simply Ta, Yiddish for "Dad."

—Schwartzie's daughter Rivka Sara Chein

Schwartzie's older children were tweens and teenagers during the years that Schwartzie began to do outreach independent of Chabad House, develop The Chai Center, and get the new project off the ground. Kids are notoriously skittish about parents who stand out from others in how they dress or how they behave. Schwartzie's kids, of course, were out of luck. They grew up in West Los Angeles with a father who not only was different from secular dads, but also was different from other *Lubavitch* dads.

For example, the rainbow suspenders. "Once I was like, 'Ta, what's with the rainbow suspenders?' They actually embarrassed me sometimes," Schwartzie's daughter Dina said at his *shloshim*, the ceremony marking thirty days after his death. "He said, 'When I was younger, I was in a boys' choir, and the cantor and the rabbi wore these tall hats and these long beards, and I was petrified. I decided that if I were ever to be a rabbi, I would wear rainbow suspenders—who would be afraid of that?' For him, it was all about connecting with others on their terms . . . This was his life mission."

Schwartzie's son, Mayshe, described Schwartzie's signature look in the 1980s: jeans, a rock 'n' roll T-shirt, a "May the force be with you" belt buckle, and a cowboy hat. "I was like, 'What's up with the dress, pops? Why can't you dress like everybody else? What's going on?'"

"I didn't understand it; I honestly didn't like it," Mayshe said. "But at the same time that I didn't like it, I kind of liked it, too. I liked being a little different; I liked being a little edgy. You know, it's like trying to have your cake and eat it, too. I enjoyed the uniqueness of it, and then at the same time, I knew I could never escape it, even if I wanted to."

Eventually, Mayshe said, Schwartzie switched to suspenders with a Mickey Mouse motif. "One time, when I was fifteen or sixteen, I asked him, 'Why do you have to wear those Mickey Mouse suspenders?'" Schwartzie gave Mayshe the same answer he had given Dina: "The reason I wear Mickey Mouse suspenders is because no one will ever be scared of a rabbi wearing Mickey Mouse suspenders."

"He was very serious when he said it," Mayshe said. "It was no joke. When my father got serious, he got serious, and it hit me like a jolt in a serious way. It wasn't a light moment; it was a heavy moment, but it was a genuine and a very real moment, and I got it. I realized, OK, now that's what he's about."

Then there were the bumper stickers. "My father had a bumper sticker collection, but that wasn't the tough part," Mayshe said. "He actually displayed the bumper sticker collection on his car, so his entire car was all full of crazy bumper stickers."

This became something of an issue when the Schwartz kids attended a well-heeled yeshiva in Los Angeles. "I would pray that my *ima* (mom) would pick me up and carpool because it was a ritzy kind of school. I was embarrassed," Mayshe related. "Sure enough, I was playing basketball one day, a Suburban rolled up, and it was bumper stickers everywhere. I looked to my friends and said, 'I've got to go. My uncle's here.'"

Mayshe also described his experiences helping his father distribute flyers for his public events during the 1980s.

> Before any big event, he would say to me, "Mayshe, we've got to put up some flyers." It didn't really appeal to me too much, but he asked in a way where you're not saying "no," so, "Yeah, of course. I'm ready. Let's do it."
>
> We put flyers up on cars all over Westwood Village. I don't think I was older than maybe eleven at the time. He would get really into it. He would say, "Hold the tape this way. Put the flyer upside-down that way. No one's gonna miss that one."

He had his "Two upside-down for sure. That's a winner right there."

Then one time, he said to me, "Mayshe, you see the 7-Eleven on the side?"

I said, "Yeah."

He went, "Run in there now."

I said, "Why?"

He said, "The cops are following us."

"What do you mean they're following us? What did we do?" I was wondering whether he was a criminal and I didn't know about it. It didn't seem to me like we were doing anything wrong. We used to do this all the time. He said, "Mayshe, go into 7-Eleven and hide behind the chips. I'll see you in five minutes."

Once we were both in the 7-Eleven, I said, "Pop, what's going on?"

He says, "It's very simple. I think it's illegal to put up flyers or posters." It was after an hour of putting up five hundred flyers. He said, "But if you're shopping in 7-Eleven and you're not in the act, chances are the cops can't really pull you over. Besides, you're a minor. They won't take you if they know you're with me." I'm thinking to myself, *I have a lot of friends who are my age. There is no way they're doing this with their fathers after school.*

At a very early age, it hit me that my father was a little different from the other dads I went to school with in the city. But I took a lot of pride in that, because first of all, when you're eleven years old, dodging cops is actually a fun thing. Getting chips and Slurpees in the process, also nice.

Years later, Mayshe said, when he was around nineteen, Schwartzie took him to a debate at Sinai Temple in Los Angeles featuring Conservative Rabbi David Wolpe and Modern Orthodox Rabbi Shmuley Boteach. The latter rabbi had published a controversial article in *Playboy* magazine, and

Schwartzie knew the event represented a more secular environment than Mayshe was used to. But Mayshe was interested in going, and Schwartzie was willing to have him there.

> To go with my father anywhere was always fun, because as soon as he'd walk into a room, there'd be a draw. Everybody would want to know who he was, hanging out with him. Those who didn't know, those who did know. You were always with this celebrity sort of status, and I was his kid, so I got to rub some of that on me, and that was always a fun thing to do.

> The fact that I was a nineteen-year-old yeshiva boy, and he would take me to this event, showed you his fearlessness; he wasn't scared. He was educating me in his own indirect way to not be scared of what could be perceived as "You should, you shouldn't." He was guided by halachah, and anything outside of that, if it could affect more Jews, he was all in.

And, of course, it was an opportunity to spread the word about The Chai Center. "He said, 'Mayshe, there are a lot of Jews here. Grab the flyers and pin all the cars.' My father sneaked out with me, and there we were, in the garage, putting flyers on cars. He saw a Rolls-Royce and said, 'Give him two. It's a Rolls. Give him two.' You had to be tricky because you could set off an alarm easily on those Mercedes and stuff like that, so it became a whole art form."

Daughter Hindel described Schwartzie as a wonderful dad who was there for his kids, calling him a father "who understood our teenage angst, our school problems, and what weren't actually problems. He didn't let us sweat the small stuff and gave us great perspective on what was actually important in the real world and what wasn't. He really never cared about our school work—as long as we were getting all As and Bs—and focused completely on our behavior toward teachers and fellow students."

Moreover, he was an equal-opportunity parent. "His love for his children was so great that nothing and no one could break that unconditional love," Hindel said. "He never compared us. There were a lot of us. He never made us feel competitive, one against the other. He just thought we were brilliant, funny, and talented. To him, we walked on water."

"We shared him with the world and yet never felt resentful, as we knew we always came first," Hindel's sister Rivka Sara said at Schwartzie's shloshim. "Maybe the exception was his older sister, Olga, who even at the age of 71 called him Baby Bobby Precious Face. Hard to compete with that. We knew that sharing him never took away from us."

Schwartzie never slept late, Hindel said, and his day began long before he drove the children to school at 7:20 every morning. He would end his workday around 9:30 p.m., his cutoff hour for making phone calls. "After 9:30 was when he would hang out in the living room, exhausted, and just be around and watch with glee the kids' interaction," Hindel recalled. "He would watch our Tetris competitions for hours. His favorite nightly line was, 'This is better than TV.' He just loved watching us play and interact."

Hindel remembers a Schwartzie who was punctual to every event and meticulous about every detail of life, from how he prepared his lunch to where people sat at parties and how many inches apart the chairs were placed. "He took hours preparing for his classes, wrote out notes and cards, and it didn't matter if he had taught that class before," Hindel said. "He always came well prepared. For years, I heard him give us kids speeches about how it was so important to the Rebbe to prepare for every class he taught."

Rivka Sara remembered the preparation for her bat mitzvah. "My father wrote the speech and made me practice with him numerous times," she said. "He underlined words in red and wrote comments in bold, like 'Pause, look up.' In one place, he even wrote, 'Take a big pause here for laughter.'"

Schwartzie was a highly public man who nevertheless prized one-on-one interaction. When dozens of people showed up for Shabbat dinner at the family home, "he would speak a few minutes and sing a few *niggunim*, and the rest of the meal was people enjoying each other's company at a Shabbat table," Hindel recalled. "But he never was fully satisfied when it was over. The meal always went too fast for him, and he was never able to make his way around the table fully before the meal was over."

Unlike Mayshe, Hindel wasn't called upon to stick flyers under windshield wipers, but from age fifteen, she was sometimes pressed into service as a receptionist at Schwartzie's singles parties. "By the time I was eighteen, he was telling me to say that I'm the rabbi's daughter so that no one would hit on me," she said. "By the time I was nineteen, I realized that line was like honey for bees, and I switched it to, 'I'm the rabbi's daughter, and I just turned fifteen.'

"Behind the scenes, he was a normal father, a normal man," Hindel said. "We would wake up Shabbat morning, his only quiet morning of the week without obligations, and he would be at the Shabbat table with books spread all around him, learning Torah. For a very public person, he really loved and needed his quiet time. But almost nobody knew this about him, because if someone were around, he would never choose the books over human interaction. I saw him many times have to close his books when people walked into the house so he could give them attention. He loved his learning, but he just didn't have lots of time to learn."

Schwartzie brought his children into his work, taking them on shiva calls and to lifecycle events, and having them make phone calls or take notes if he was confined to bed with a bad back. But many Sundays were work days just for him. "Sunday often was a beach day for us, with dad meeting us at the end of the day in Venice, joining us and Ima for a hot dog dinner at sunset," Hindel said.

"One of his regrets in life was not spending more time with us as kids. I had this conversation with him in my thirties. He was shocked to hear that I had no clue what he was talking about. I always felt he was available when I needed and figured this is how families function. But I know that he regretted not spending as much time as he had wanted to while we were growing up. He was focused on his mission of bringing Jews closer to Judaism and made choices that many times took him away from family time. To his dying day, I told him that he was a more present dad than many dads who were present!"

Dina reported that her father said to her more than once, "What did I do to deserve such amazing children? And how did I get so lucky that all my married kids so far are blessed to marry their bashert? And you know why I'm the richest person in the world? All these fabulous grandkids. I am the luckiest man."

As far as Dina could tell, she and her brothers and sisters were blessed and lucky, too.

Aura Schwartz Rosenblatt: A Unique Childhood

I always think of myself as having grown up with a charmed childhood. Even though being one of twelve children, with a rabbi and *rebbetzin* as parents, is not often what fairy tales are made of, I loved that my childhood was unique and far from the average life of a kid in California during the 1980s and '90s.

I have always been asked what it was like growing up in my busy home and having Schwartzie as a father. And the one answer I always come back to is . . . *great!* There was never a dull moment! Our house was always full, *literally* full. It made no difference that there were twelve of us children: we always made room for one more sleepover guest and one more—okay, fine, and one more. Many Friday nights, I would find myself sleeping on the floor of my parents' room with three or more siblings, as our rooms had been given to Shabbat guests visiting from Israel, India, or just the other side of town. And I truly enjoyed the action. Of course, in my teenage years, when I just wanted space to come home Fridays and sleep or read my magazines, I may have given attitude to anyone in my line of sight. But even so, every week, I would set the table with my brothers (who joined in after much coaxing).

And then Friday night would roll around, and fifty or more people would come for Shabbat dinner. It was exciting every week. We had some regulars who became family, and then there were the constant new strangers of all ages and all walks of life. I observed my parents greeting everyone with the same warm smile and genuine love for their fellow Jew. I am known to have the "gift of gab," and though I believe this comes naturally, I most certainly learned how to speak to everyone and anyone with warmth and kindness from my parents. I watched my father entertain new and old friends on our porch, which overlooked the entire city.

The sights are still so clear to me. The Los Angeles sky streaked with orange, yellow, and pink as the city lights emerged quietly at first and then brightly, as the sun gave way to night. A burned-out match lying on the floor near the Shabbat candles that were just lit by my mother and all the women. Schwartzie's Mickey Mouse watch keeping track of the time that everyone else seemed to be losing as they enjoyed their conversation at the "shmooze and cruise" happy hour.

Shabbat was so special in our home in a genuine way! I learned that it doesn't matter if you have fancy china dishes and crystal, or paper plates and Dixie cups—people are drawn to learning, growing, and just enjoying the comfort of a home-cooked meal and good conversation, which sometimes does more for a person's soul than anything else.

My life with my father expanded far beyond the weekend. He taught me from the time I was young about confidence and independence. My father never failed to tell me and my sisters how beautiful we were. I guess I have even adopted that trait in my adult life, as sometimes my husband will jokingly point out that I beat him to the compliment as I look in the mirror and tell myself, "Wow, I look good!"

But the most important part of this self-confidence goes deeper than beauty. My father taught us to take our self-confidence with us in all aspects of life, from believing we can get whichever job we wanted, to standing up for ourselves and others against any naysayers. Confidence also enables all of us to have meaningful relationships with our spouses, children, and friends, and that inheritance is priceless.

One of my favorite traits I learned from my father is loyalty—loyalty to oneself, friends, and especially siblings! In our house, no one was allowed to be a tattletale. We learned how to work out conflicts on our own and get along. He encouraged our individual relationships with one another, and in turn, he gave us an in-house support group that money can't buy.

We learned to trust our instincts and, consequently, our father trusted us. On my sixteenth birthday, I got my driver's license. It was a Friday, and, of course, an hour after receiving said license, I was picking up carpool and going to the grocery store for my folks.

Naturally, Saturday night I was ready to use my license to go out with my friends. There was one problem. My mother and I were having a disagreement about a curfew: she thought I should have a curfew, and I most definitely didn't want one. We went back and forth for a bit and finally my father said, "What time do the bars close, 2 a.m.?! OK, your curfew is 2 a.m." He appreciated all the errands and carpools I would be helping with, and he showed that appreciation by trusting me.

My father always joked that his kids didn't talk to him from their teenage years until they were in their twenties or married. For the most part, that was true, though I believe it's true in many parent-child relationships. In my early twenties, I started asking for Ta's advice again. When I moved to New York for the second time, it was difficult for me. My father quoted a Jewish proverb, "All new beginnings are difficult," and he added that it makes you a stronger person. Which, of course, it did.

When I started dating, he advised, "Let the guy pursue you." I took that to heart, and my husband, Dov, called me for six weeks before I agreed to go on a date with him. Eleven happy years later, Ta's advice was clearly the right advice.

There is so much about my father that I miss: his unconditional love toward me and my family, his love of life, his love for Israel and the Jewish people, and his respect for his Rebbe. But I will truly miss the days we got to spend together in the last couple of years. We had some special heart-to-heart conversations and great belly laughs. And he was always ready to listen to whatever it was I was gabbing about that day.

I am honored to follow in his footsteps in so many ways, and I know—because he gave me the confidence to know—that he is eternally proud of me.

CHILD #10 SHMULLY SCHWARTZ:
SO MANY SPECIAL TIMES

Schwartzie was known for a lot of things: Jewish Astrology on Venice Beach, hundreds of weddings, singles parties for Jews, his Mickey Mouse watch and suspenders—and his character. But I remember especially the High Holidays, Passover, Chanukah, and making Shabbat on Friday night.

Friday night was an event. My mom had to cook for about fifty people. That means she usually started making the bread and *tahine* Thursday evening. My dad would make phone calls throughout the week inviting people. We had the regulars: Ronny, Ben, Jeff, Yasmine, Joan. These people could pop in anytime, no reservation needed. The others had to be invited. Growing up, at times I felt neglected, or, to be more accurate, left alone, but I never thought about having my parents to myself on the weekend. Friday night was fun for us.

We had to set the table after we came home from school on Friday, and then I would go with my dad to Venice Beach to put up flyers for whatever event was coming up. There was such a hustle and bustle in the house on Friday, with my sister playing her early nineties rap music, Cuisinart machines scratching the inside of your ears, some kids playing basketball outside with the ball smashing against the window every fourth shot. But when Friday night came, it was peaceful. My dad would hold court on the upstairs patio, and my mom would take a quick rest in her room. Music was turned off, and we stopped fighting with each other.

Once all thirty-plus guests were packed into the patio, my mom would ask me to count how many people were up there. Often she would say, "What, how are there fifty people when I only invited twenty?!" Well, if my dad invited fifty but told her only twenty were coming, then there was a simple answer to that question, but I didn't say anything. After everyone had shuffled to their seats, my dad would sing "*Shalom Aleichem.*" Usually I was in the kitchen enjoying the elbow room until I had to go sit down.

I remember my dad saying, "Now we're going to bless the wine." He had a red beard, bald head, stood about five foot seven, though as a kid I thought he was closer to six feet, and had a nice belly. He was always proud to say of his physique, "I haven't been 180 pounds since high school!" Meaning, becoming svelte ain't happening. When he got sick, that was probably his biggest concern. "How can I be 160 pounds?" he would ask. I think it brought home how sick he really was.

Friday night, he'd be standing at the head of the table. We'd have the main dining table at the head of the room and three folding tables against it, forming an E shape. My mom's candles sparkled in some corner of the room. Plasticware by each seat with a folding chair against it. All types of people: old, young, middle-aged, kids, tattooed, religious sleep-over guests, long-haired, no hair, suited, tie-dyed, nose rings, and everything in between. The light was soft, and the night was the cool LA kind. My father would start the blessing: "On the sixth day, after the heavens and earth were created . . ." That was Shabbat.

* * *

Many people ask my siblings and me, and if they don't, they should, how we are all so close with one another, how we all are so confident, caring, loving, and genuine with each other and with most people who cross our paths. To be honest, it's a mystery. I mean, we got a few things that are needed to create a tight-knit family, but there was some craziness, too, which should have offset all that.

The first thing that we got from my mom, Olivia, and dad, Schwartzie, was unconditional love. My mom always exclaimed, "You're so handsome," and my dad told me growing up, "You're one of my smartest children." It was more than that, though. I think they just liked us more than everyone else. My dad would spend more time with people he was counseling or getting to know, the groupies and his actual friends, than with us, but we knew he liked us better than all of them, even if he didn't show it with quality time. Of course, it would have been nice to see him more, but I understood his work was spending time with other people, bringing them closer to Judaism, and that was always the first order of the day.

His favorite time of year was the High Holidays. He loved the shofar blowing during the month of Elul, the mailing he would send out, speaking to the hotel where we were having the services, and most of all, speaking to the two-thousand-plus Jews who would come over the course of the next few weeks. We all helped in one way or another—shlepping boxes, stuffing envelopes, putting up flyers, cooking for the family—and having to behave because it was a serious time of year.

Thinking back on all of this makes me wonder how we all turned out so normal. It's not a common thing for an eight-year-old to be preparing a hotel ballroom for nine hundred people to sit in, pray, connect, and have a brochure to take home so we can keep in touch the rest of the year.

Uncommon was one of my dad's guiding principles. It earned him celebrity status, but more importantly, which I didn't realize growing up, it allowed him to be the sort of rabbi he wanted to be. He kept a few of the basic rules, like no handshakes with women, strict kosher and Sabbath observance, but he did it all in T-shirts and jeans.

I remember one year he was exhausted after standing on the stage for five hours and had to sit down in the front row once the services had concluded. Many people would come over to say a quick hello, or a long hello if they weren't socially aware, and he would smile at all of them and wish them a happy new year. I remember his sitting down and then looking up to see whom he needed to speak to. There'd be about twenty people huddled around him with some forming a line waiting to say hello. The auditorium that year was a big theater in Beverly Hills, with long rows of seats and a stage with a massive blue curtain covering the screen. My dad's long beard was graying, and he was wearing a crisp button-down shirt, black pants, and black Nike Airs. It was the only time of year he would really dress up.

My dad could be loud and boisterous, but after a High Holidays service, he was soft-spoken. I think he was proud of a job well done.

MESSAGES TO AND FROM THE NEXT WORLD

September 2017

Dear Father,

It's been a few months since you passed to the higher world on February 8, 2017.

To the world, you were Schwartzie. To me, you were just father.

With a few days to go before the High Holidays, I am preparing notes and stories to inspire two thousand of our Jews, *your* Jews, who will attend your services at the Writers Guild Theater in Beverly Hills, Jews who are not affiliated with any other temple or Jewish denomination.

From the time I was a child, I watched you on stage, conducting services with the cantor and the "Schwartz Tabernacle Choir." I watched you entertain and dazzle the crowd. I remember comics from the Laugh Factory coming to you after services and saying, "Schwartzie, how do you have enough script to hold the crowd for eight hours? I can barely do eight minutes at the club!"

I remember your High Holidays services in 1989, where you coined the term "Don't Pay to Pray." People didn't believe such a service was possible. We didn't have a minyan that morning. You asked me to fetch a tenth person so we could start services. I was cute and young with curly hair. Who can say no to a 13-year-old child? How far we've come. You've filled the Bonaventure Hotel, the Pantages Theater, and now the theater at the Writers Guild of America. You've done well, father.

I remember you sitting in your wheelchair on stage last Yom Kippur reciting the *Shehecheyanu,* thanking G-d that he granted you life till that point. I remember leading the service last year as you sat in your white robe fasting, not taking your meds against all your doctors' orders. I was happy you were there, coaching me, motioning to me, prodding me, telling me to insert another joke.

I will miss you this year on stage, father. I will miss not feeling your hands on my head before Yom Kippur as you blessed me the first forty years of my life.

Your son,
Mendel

Dear Son,

The shiva has passed. And the thirty-day shloshim has passed. Now is the time to be happy and stand upright. Now is the time for you to perform and conduct yourself like the rabbi that I taught you to be for forty years. I am up here with a fabulous crowd of people, and we're all looking down at you. I am here with the Baal Shem Tov and the Lubavitcher Rebbe who gave me my career, and who taught us not to be afraid and to love every single Jew regardless of observance or affiliation. We are all excited to watch you on stage. We know you'll be inspiring, and we hope to hear some new jokes. But go ahead and use some of my old material.

Remember the story of the Klausenberger Rebbe, Yekusiel Yehudah Halberstam, who was born in 1905 and passed away in 1994? His wife and eleven children were killed during the Holocaust. He was as strong as a lion, even though all his loved ones passed. Even General Dwight Eisenhower came to meet him in 1945 in a displaced persons camp in Munich, Germany, to witness this great rabbi. He was so strong, he later remarried and had an additional seven children.

In 1946, before Yom Kippur, a nine-year-old orphan came to his tent in the DP camp and asked the Rebbe to bless him since he had no father. The Rebbe graciously agreed. Word got out that the Rebbe blessed this orphan, and within a few minutes all the orphans started to line up and receive a blessing from the Rebbe. One by one, the Rebbe blessed ninety kids. Only once the last child was blessed did the Rebbe begin the Kol Nidrei.

Before the Rebbe passed in 1994, his students asked, "Who will be our Rebbe after your passing?" And the Rebbe answered, "All the Jews who light the Shabbat candles before sunset, and all the Jews who put on tefillin, they will be your Rebbe. They will be your guide and inspiration."

So, my son Mendel, I am wearing my tie-dyed T-shirt, and I am next to the Klausenberger Rebbe, who is wearing his white button-down shirt and black fur hat. And we both agree that this year, although I am not with you physically to bless you this Yom Kippur, you should look at the crowd sitting in the Writers Guild theater. Look at the thousand Jews who chose not to watch a Netflix show, but chose to attend services. They chose to listen to you as their new rabbi. They chose to listen as you will rattle off my ten suggestions to keep the Jewish people stronger. They are your new Rebbe. They are the new FOUNDING FATHERS AND MOTHERS of the Jewish people.

Am Yisroel Chai and Shanah Tovah,

Your father,
Schwartzie

ACKNOWLEDGMENTS

No one puts together a book all by himself, and for a project like this one, which involves real people telling true stories and combines research, interviews, and the perusal of hundreds of documents, you need a small army of contributors, supporters, wordsmiths, and technicians. In this space, I express my gratitude to some of the people who helped the most in realizing my father's vision.

Family first: I must thank my mother, Olivia Schwartz, who was my father's partner (and, to a degree, his manager) for almost 40 years, and my brother Rabbi Mayshe Schwartz for providing insight to this book. My brother-in-law Rabbi Yaakov Shallman was instrumental throughout the entire process of gathering material for and putting together the book, from the first interview to the final details. Yaakov was at my side for months, hashing out many tough issues that needed definitive answers. My cousin Ron Reisman, the Schwartz family's unofficial archivist, provided numerous digitally preserved photographs, along with documents of our family's move from Europe to the United States. Uncle Avraham Deitsch contributed dates and other information about the Deitsch family. And all my other siblings get a special shout-out for cheering me on. From the top: Chanale, Shaya, Rick, Hindel, Dina, Yos, Aura, Shmu, Berry, and Cobe.

Many, many friends of Schwartzie's, some going back to the 1950s, provided invaluable firsthand testimony about Schwartzie's youth, his years at UCLA and Cal State Northridge, and his activities within and outside the CHAI Center in the form of interviews, written accounts, and videos. There are too many to list individually, but I do want to single out Dr. Steve Bailey, a boyhood Atlantic City pal who stayed in touch with Schwartzie throughout their lives, and Dr. Mark Lustman, Schwartzie's best friend from Talmudical Academy; each contributed stories and facts from their school years with Schwartzie. Thanks also go to Shtul and Ruchie Stillman, who clarified stories and dates from Schwartzie's Westwood days and brought calm to the many Schwartz children.

From the CHAI Center, I need to acknowledge Vicky Judah, who began interviewing Schwartzie and transcribing all his stories when he was compiling material himself for a memoir; Rivkie Blau, Schwartzie's personal assistant for 10 years; and Dina Shallman, for building the Schwartzie Legacy website at www.chaicenter.org/schwartzie. I am also grateful to Dr. David Katzin and Lily Goldfarb, two people who have made commitments of love and finances to the CHAI Center since its genesis, in addition to contributions toward the personal well-being of the Schwartz family for many years and support for this book.

Many thanks go to the team at Business Ghost that produced this book: CEO Michael Levin, who helped conceptualize the book and conducted interviews for it; Rabbi Ellen Jaffe-Gill, who turned hundreds of disparate documents and transcripts into an insightful and colorful narrative; editor-in-chief Bryan Gage; and publishing coordinator Rebecca Frost.

I must give special acknowledgment to my wife, Esther, mother of our six children, who kept me strong and upright, especially through Schwartzie's last years. Esther, may you continue to lead the next generation of young singles and millennials and keep them connected to their faith.

Finally, thank you to our 500-plus contributors who donated $5.00 or more when we ran the "Schwartzie Campaign" to launch this book in February 2017, with special mention to Dudi and Chanie Farkash for their contribution.

SCHWARTZIE CAMPAIGN CONTRIBUTORS

Mr. & Mrs. Charles Abehsera, Mr. & Ms. Chuck Abel, Rabbi & Mrs. Aaron Abend, Rabbi Nachman Abend, Rakefet Abergel, Mr & Mrs Yakov Abergel, Karen Admon, Adam Aftergut, Mr. Jila Ahdot, Mr. Sam Alter, Josh & Tova Altmann, Mr. & Mrs. Jonathan Anschell, Mr & Mrs Bob Arkin, Mr. Ron Ascher, Ms. Yocheved Baitelman, Kathryn Barash, Fradel Barber, Mr. Michael Barclay, Howard & Becky Baron, Menachem Baron, Jayme B. Barrett, Ms Lisa Barroll, Rick Barzilli, Mr. Steve Bass, Mr. & Mrs. Shea Bastomski, Rabbi Dovi Begun, Yaacov Behrman, Levi Benjaminson, Rabbi Mendel Bernstein, Sharone & Theresa Bershatski, Paul Bilski, Mr. Aaron Biston, Chili Biston, Rabbi & Mrs Shlomo Bistritzky, Mr. & Mrs. Joshua Bittan, Mr. Allen Black, Stanley Black, Dr. Mindy Boxer, Dr. & Mrs. Theo Brandt-Sarif, Janice Brenman, Asa Bright, Bonnie Brodsky, Chaim Shaul & Raizel Brook, Helen Brown, Rabbi Chaim Bruk, Zev Brummel, Chaim & Shula Bryski, Chaim Binyomin & Chana Baila Burston, Dahlia Cantor, Phivel Caplan, Civia Caroline, Dr David Caroline, David Case, Chanoch Chaskind, Mendel & Rivka Sara Chein, Rabbi Mordechai Chein, Lori Coburn, Mr. & Mrs. Mike Cofsky, Mr. Harvey Cogen, Carrie Cohen, Mr. Daniel Cohen, Danny Cohen, Ethan Cohen, Ira R. & Linda Cohen, Mr. & Mrs. Leslie Cohen, Lynne Cohen, Motti & Devora Leah Cohen, Paul & Kathy Cohen, Sofi Cohen, Wayne & Elizabeth Cohen, Aliza Coren, Karen Corwin, Lee & Wendy Crystal, Rabbi Chaim Cunin, Tzemach Cunin, Rabbi Yossi Cunin, Gayle Damiano, Dr. & Mrs. Alan Dauer, Eli & Rochel Deitsch, Rabbi & Mrs Mendy Deitsch, Mordecai Deitsch, Rabbi & Mrs Nechemia Deitsch, Sholom Y. & Chanale Deitsch, Ms. Robin Dubowitz, Zalmi & Leah Duchman, Yossi Eber, Ari Edelman, Mr. & Mrs. Yoel S. Edelson, Nancy Edelstein, Eli Eichenblatt, Mr. & Mrs. Yehudit Eichenblatt, Rabbi Mordy Einbinder, Mr. & Mrs. Scott Einbinder, Rabbi & Mrs Shlomo Einhorn, Mr. & Mrs. Shmuel Einstein, Sava Kim Ellis, Dr & Mrs. Shlomo Leib Elspas, Faiga Engel, Joshy Engelson, Mr Marc Erlbaum, Miriam M. Eshaghian-Wilner, Dr. & Ms. Bruce B. Ettinger, Rami Even-Esh, Jana Falic, Lisa Falic-Groisman, Michael & Tanya Farah, Duddy & Chani Farkash, Mordechai Farkash, Yitzhak Farkash, Mr. & Mrs. Richard Fauman, Leonid & Elvira Favelyukis, Robin Federman, Sholom Feigelstock, Mr. & Mrs. Yisroel Feiner, Rabbi Edward M. Feinstein, Kenneth Feinstein, Gershon & DL Felberbaum, Shalom Feldman, Deborah Fellman, Rachel Ferency, Yehuda & Miriam Ferris, Natan Ferszt, Tzvi & Rivka Ferszt, Ms. Elaine Fidel, Eileen Finizza, Daniel & Romy Fishman, Debra Fletcher, Rocky & Danielle Forer, B.L. Manger Foundation, Rabbi & Mrs. Yonah Fradkin, John & Susan Frankel, Ms. Sandra Frankel, Marlene Frantz, Marcus Freed, Judy Freier, Mr & Mrs Chaim Friedman, Rabbi & Mrs Eli Friedman, Mendel & Chaya Friedman, Rabbi & Mrs Yuda Friedman, Mr & Mrs Rod Fryer, Tamar Gabriel, Daniel Ganjian, Bentzion Geisinsky, Meir Geisinsky, Mr Velvel Geisinsky, Jeff & Terry Gelb, Ilona Geller, Rabbi Laura Geller, Mr. Henri Gerber, Karen Gersten, Lisa Gewirtz, Eli & Ruthy Ginsburg, Mr. & Mrs. Gregg Gittler, Julie Given, Gail Glaser, Mr. & Mrs. Paul Glassman, Milton & Raizy Goffman, Jeff Gold, Dalia Goldbarb-Waysman, Joe & Hilla Goldberg, Mr. & Mrs. Mark Goldenberg, Lily Berman Goldfarb, Mr. & Mrs. Sol Goldner, Eileen Golestani, Ms. Cathy L. Goodman, Raphael Goorevitch, Yossi Gordon, Rabbi & Dr. Mel Gottlieb, Ms Irina Govlich, Stephen S. Graham, Joan Marks, Richard G. & Barbara Granatt, Ms. Trudy Green, Boruch & Roza Greenbaum, Yehoshua Greenberg, Miri Greenwald, Devorah Groner, Levi Groner, Arielle Gross, Mr. & Mrs. Jeff Grunfeld, Mr Michael Hager, William & Orly Halac, Yonatan & Rivka Sara Hambourger, Dr. Lisa Hannifin, Chaya Tova Hartman, Sharona Hassidim, Shifra Hastings, Devorah Hayman, Marvin Hershenson, David & Dodie Herskovitz, Sara & Talia Hess, Cheryl Himmelstein, Levi Hodakov, Bernard & Gal Hoffman, Yechiel Hoffman, Aryeh Hurwitz, Rabbi Yitzi Hurwitz, Levi Illulian, Ms. Lynda J. Jackson, Miss Marcia Jacobs, Howard Jacobson, Mr & Mrs Howard Jacobson, Ms. Rochel leah Jaffe, Mr. Dovid Kagan, Eli Kagan, Mr Nashi Kagan, Mr. & Mrs. Simcha Kagan, Tamar Kagan, Dr. & Mrs. David Kalmanson, Stacy Kamin, Mr. Gary Kamisher, Rabbi Yehuda Kantor, Marisashi Katz, Mordechai Katz, Richard Katz, Dr David Katzin, Sara Katzman, Andrea Kaufman, Mr. & Mrs. Ronald Kaufman, Ms. Andrea F. Kelly, Rabbi Moshe Kesselman, Sara Khansari, Inessa Kibrik, Ariel & Chenya Kimhi, Judy Kitchner, Daniel & Robyn Klasner, Avigail Klein, Schneur Klyne, Chaim Kohn, Daniel & Leigh Kohn, Shmuli & Mimi Kopfstein, Rabbi & Mrs Shmully Kornfeld, Ami & Rozy Kozak, Shalom & Kayla Kramer, Andrew Krasnow, Joy Krauthammer, Chanie Kravitz, Tzvi & Shana Kravitz, Janet Krost, Michael & Casey Krubiner, Menachem Kudan, Vadim & Dianna Kuraev, Lorraine J Laby, Pini Lackner, Pamela Lane, Rabbi & Mrs. Josef Langer, Miss Patti Lavine, Mr. Allen Lazarus, Rivka Leah, Steven & Jodi Leanse, Ilene Gay Leeds MFT, Rom & Ariella Leibner, Levi Leider, Rabbi Moshe Leider, Nechama Dina Lein, Donna Leskly, Ms. Marla Leventhal, Michal Danny Levin, Fayge Levin, Moshe Levin, Dr. & Dr. Allan Levine, Mirel Levitansky, Martin Levy, Menashe Levy, Shmuel & Rivky Levy, Rabbi Yosef Lew, Dr David Liberman, Steven Liberman, Levy Lieberman, Stanley Lieberman, Sheldon & Alejandra Linderman, Matt Lipeles, Philip Lipp, Rabbi Chaim Lipskar, Avi & Sarah Lipsker, Rabbi Leibel Lipsker, Yossi & Gila Lipsker, Rabbi Zalman & Mariam Lipskier, Chaim Lisbon, Mendel & Chana Golda Lisbon, Allen Lissauer, Mr. & Mrs. Elie Litov, Mr. & Mrs. Sal Litvak, Mr Mordchai Loksen, Devorah Loschak, Gary Lustgarten, Dr. & Mrs. Mark Lustman, Howard N. Madris, Chaim Mahgel, Chaya Hinda Malka, Mr. Barry Mallin, Lori Clarity Mandel, Yana & Jonothon Marcelino, Yana Yakubsfeld, Rabbi Zalman Marcus, Zeesh (Eli) Marcus, Michael Margolese, Michal Taviv, Miss Stephen Mark, Mr. & Mrs. Brad Markoff, Ahron & Sara Markovitch, Choni & Frumie Marozow, Cheryl Marquart, Mr. Jaime Mas, Micky & Jessica Mayerson, Feiga Mazer, David Mazouz, Bernard & Marilyn Mendoza, Noi Meschaninov, Mr Ilya Meshchaninov, Philleen Meskin, Mr. & Mrs. Herbert Meyers, Danielle Michaels, Shana Miller, Dr. & Mrs. Rubie Minkowitz, Douglas Mirell, Laurie Levenson, Mr. & Mrs. Yosef Mishulovin, Cheston & Lara Mizel, Joseph Mizrachi, Yaakov Mizrachi, Elisheva Mochkin, Peretz & Miryum Mochkin, Erez & Sigal E. Moler, David Morris, Jacob & Lynn Moskowitz, Rabbi & Mrs Dov Muchnik, Shneur & Zavie Munitz, Yis Munitz, Mr. Dovid Nagel, Bernie/Berel Nagler, Rabbi & Mrs. Shmuel Naparstek, Rabbi Reuven Nathanson, Yossi & Yael Nathanson, Devorah Natkin, Ms. Marsha Nelson, Shawn A. & Kristin Nelson, Shalom & Cherry New, Dr. & Ms. Saul Newman, Ms. Melinda Nicholson, Beatrice Nudelman, Itzik & Tani Nureali, Suzanne Okin, Aryeh Orloff, Yossi & Shaina Palace, Laurie Parker, Ms. Shirley Perl, Mr. & Mrs. Shelly Perluss, Ms. Linda Perry, Mr & Mrs Neil

Pershin, Mr David Albert Pierce, Yossi & Devorah Pinson, Darren Pitzele, Mr. & Mrs. Elozor Plotke, Mendel Plotke, Mr. & Mrs. Avrohom Plotkin, Mr. & ` Jack Podolski, Mr. & Mrs. Richard Polak, Marty Pollack, Phyllis Pollack, Brock & Natalia Pollock, Estee Posin, Eli & Ita Posner, Seth Potter, Richard Press, Theodore L Press, Orna Rachovitsky, Yecheskel Raeburn, Mr. & Mrs. Saul Raigorodsky, Robby Rajber, Mr & Mrs Russell Rapoport, Ms Shana Rapoport, Ezzy Rappaport, Mitch & Atara Reichman, Mr. Bruce Reinauer, Mr. Ron Reisman, Mr. & Mrs. Frank Revere, Andrew & Shoshanna Rhein, Mr. & Mrs. Meir Rhodes, Mr. Dan Robbins, Brenda Robin, Shira Roman, Mr. & Mrs. Daniel Romm, Dr. & Mrs. Eli Rosen, Chaya Rosenberg, Marilyn Rosenberger, Dov Rosenblatt, Aura Schwartz, Jason Rosenblatt, Mr & Mrs Batya Rosenblum, Mr. & Mrs. Robert Rosenblum, Devorah Leah Rosenfeld, Mrs Yaakov Rosenthal, Rivka Chaya Rossi, Richard & Rahla Kahn Rossner, Mr Aaron Roth, Avrohom Roth, Gerald Roth, Miss Janna Roth, Yossi & Rivkah Roth, Miss Andrea Rubin, Rabbi & Mrs. Chaim B. Rubin, Ms. Nina Rubin, Tamar Rubin, Ariella Ruderman, Sean Rudes, Mr. & Mrs. Reuvane Russell, Jessie Rutiz, Zvi Ryzman, Mendel S, Ms Shella Sadovnik, Erez & Nina Safar, Miss Regina Safdie, Dr. Donald J. Salzberg, Mr. Lee Samson, Rabbi & Mrs. Yitzchak Sapo, Mark & Karen Sarto, Susan Sarto, Joy Schechter, Juda Schloss, Wendy Schneider, Chaim & Pesha Rivka Schochet, Mr. & Mrs Don Scholl, Sarah Chana Schreiber, Eliyahu & Dena Schusterman, Ezzy & Nechama Schusterman, Carl Schwaber, Menachem Schwei, Mendel Segal, Jacob & Dina Shallman, Mr. & Mrs. Jon Sher, Yitzchok & Rochel Shlomo, Sruli & Aliza Shochet, Vladimir Shtern, Barbara Shulman, Mrs Dalia Shusterman, Todd Shyres, Bonnie Siegal, Mr. & Mrs. Aryeh Siegel, Mordechai Siev, Mr. & Mrs. Neil Silverstein, Avrohom Simon, Craig & Edva Sims, David Smith, Mr. & Mrs. Gregory Smith, Rabbi Naftali Smith, Larry Smoller, Sandee Smoller, Dr Yaakov Sollins, Resha Solomon, Yehuda & Naomi Solomon, Isaac Jack & Elka Soussana, Asi Spiegel, Ben & Jill Spielman, Dr. & Mrs. Jose Spiwak, Rochel Sputz, Daniel & Diana Sragowicz, Susan Stein, Mr Daniel G. Steinberg, Ryan Steiner, Mr. & Mrs. Yrachmiel Stillman, Gerry Stober, Ms. Tammy Stockfish, Sheva Stolik, Boruch & Chaya Leah Sufrin, Dr. Jeff Sugar, Ms. Deane Swick, Yosef & Hinda Swird, Laibel & Miriam Swirdlov, Howard & Helen Szabo, David & Linda Tashman, Ezra Teitelbaum, Mr. & Mrs. Martin Teitelbaum, Aron Teleshevsky, Carmen Tellez, Bryna Telsner, Mordechai & Shuffi Telsner, Rabbi Alter Tenenbaum, Yerachmiel & Sharon Tilles, Ian & Lisa Tofler, Boaz & Cyndi Topol, Avraham Arya & Rachel Trugman, Mishael & Keren Vardi, Mr. & Mrs. Larry E. Verbit, RL Vider, Arlene Vinnick, Mr. & Mrs. Mike Volk, Yossi & Sariti Wachtel, Dov Wagner, Boruch Waldman, Eli & Shula Wasserman, Stuie & Enny Wax, Miss Teresa Waxer, Matthew & Melissa Weinberg, Mr. & Mrs. Lewis Weinger, Mr Todd Weinger, Mr. & Mrs. Nathan Weiselman, Mailech & Chana Weiss, Martin & Howard Weiss, Stephen M. Weiss, Miss Sura Lynd Weiss, David Friedman & Gabrielle M. Wenig, Mordchai & Chana Werde, Ari & Shaina Wiess, Susan Williams, Benjy Winter, Shoshana Wirtschafter, Mr. & Mrs. Baruch Wolf, Reuven & Frumy Wolf, Greg Yaris, Rabbi & Mrs. Amitai Yemini, Mr Yaakov Yemini, Daphna Zago, Rabbi & Mrs. Avraham Zajac, Sylvia Zak, Franklin Zalman, Efraim Zaltzman, Shneur Zaltzman, Yehuda & Sara Zavdi, Sherry Zelickson, Ari & Helene Zeltzer, Naor & Fabiana Zifferman, Dr & Dr Stephen Zilberbailey, Steve & Barbara Zipp, Oreet Zohar, Barry Zoller, Shellie Zuckerman, Yocheved Zuntz